SHARING THE PROPHETS

Andrew Phillips
Philip Jenkins

Sharing the Prophets
ISBN: 978-0-89098-939-5

©2023 by 21st Century Christian
4108 Hillsboro Pike, Nashville, TN 37215
All rights reserved.

All rights reserved. No part of this publication may be reproduced, stored in a retrieval system, or transmitted in any form or by any means—electronic, mechanical, photocopy, recording, digital, or otherwise—without the written permission of the publisher.

Unless otherwise indicated, all Scripture quotations are taken from The ESV® Bible (The Holy Bible, English Standard Version®), copyright © 2001 by Crossway, a publishing ministry of Good News Publishers. Used by permission. All rights reserved.

Scripture quotations marked (NASB) are taken from the New American Standard Bible® (NASB), Copyright © 1960, 1962, 1963, 1968, 1971, 1972, 1973, 1975, 1977, 1995 by The Lockman Foundation. Used by permission.
www.Lockman.org

Scripture quotations marked (NIV) are taken from the Holy Bible, New International Version®, NIV®. Copyright © 1973, 1978, 1984, 2011 by Biblica, Inc.™ Used by permission of Zondervan. All rights reserved worldwide. www.zondervan.com The "NIV" and "New International Version" are trademarks registered in the United States Patent and Trademark Office by Biblica, Inc.™

Cover design by Brent Bruce

Table of Contents

Chapter 1	Nathan: The Truth-Telling Prophet	7
Chapter 2	Elijah: The Fiery Prophet	15
Chapter 3	Elisha: A Prophet with Perspective	23
Chapter 4	Isaiah: The Volunteer Prophet	31
Chapter 5	Jeremiah: The Weeping Prophet	39
Chapter 6	Ezekiel: The "Prop-phet"	47
Chapter 7	Daniel: The Almost Prey, Always Praying Prophet	55
Chapter 8	Hosea: The Prophet Who Married a Prostitute	63
Chapter 9	Jonah: The Fish Food Prophet	71
Chapter 10	Micah: The Justice-Seeking Prophet	79
Chapter 11	Habakkuk: The Prophet with Messy Questions	87
Chapter 12	John: The Baptizing Prophet	93
Chapter 13	Anna: The Prophetess with Enduring Faith	101

Sharing the Prophets

Introduction

From Philip…

I confess to you: I believe I have been guilty of ignoring the prophets.

Typing that startles me a little bit. After all, ignoring the prophets was about the worst thing their audience could have done, for in doing so, they were ignoring not only the messengers of God, but the very messages of God.

Most of us have gotten to be pretty good at ignoring things that we don't like to hear, and that's exactly what people did with the prophets. After all, it is much easier to brush God's truth aside to than to change because change requires sacrifice.

Isn't it amazing what God will show us if only we will take the time to see? Now I see why the prophets are so revered. Now I see why it truly was a compliment for Jesus to be compared to them. Now I see why Jesus himself was able to identify with them. After all, He met the same fate as many of them: rejection, persecution, and death.

Although that approach might've worked in the past, what Jesus' opponents would learn is that they couldn't kill this One—He was more than a prophet. If only the Pharisees hadn't ignored the prophets, they, too, would've seen that Jesus was the very One about whom the prophets foretold: the Suffering Servant, the Righteous Branch, the coming King.

The Son of God.

Sharing the Prophets

It is with great pleasure that Andrew and I present to you "Sharing the Prophets," a study designed to introduce you to some peculiar, bold, determined, lackluster, lonely, convicted, entertaining, stubborn, miserable, hopeful, burden-bearing, willing, unwilling, obedient, disobedient messengers of God. In some ways, we are nothing like them, but in others, we are alike.

This book is dedicated to my wife, Laura, who makes a habit of listening to God. She is my hero, and I'm thankful that our children, Lucas and Holley, get to have her as their momma.

From Andrew...

Prophets had tough jobs. This book focuses on several prophets from different points in history and various books of the Bible, but some common threads tie them together. For instance, they had to stand up against oppressive cultures set against God, but they also had to stand up to God's people who were not living for Him. When we teach in our teen Bible classes, we must do both those things. We have to equip our young people to stand for God no matter what our surrounding culture might say, and we must also hold Christians accountable for living God's way.

It is my prayer that this book can help teens think critically about their own faith development and what it takes to serve God.

This book is dedicated to my wife, Kathryn, who has taught me a great deal about love, encouragement, and faithfulness, and to my sons, Luke and Micah, who have blessed our lives in more ways than I can count.

Mystery Item: COMPASS

Every week, we will give you an object to associate with the prophet so that you can remember something important about him or her.

Say something like:
When I say "Nathan," I want you to remember "compass."

What do you think Nathan has to do with a compass? Any theories out there?

What does a compass do? It always points north. When you lose your way, it helps you find how to get back where you need to be. Nathan acted as a compass to David, who was caught up in a web of lies. Because of his influence, he was able to play a significant role in helping David find his way back to where he needed to be—right in the eyes of God.

Ice Breakers

Option 1: The Elephant in the Room
Walk into class with something obviously wrong about your appearance. It might be toothpaste all around the edges of your mouth, a large piece of spinach stuck between your teeth, or the fact that you're wearing two completely different shoes.

Ask your students to share with you something good about their week and see how long it takes them to say something about your appearance (surely one of them will have the guts or lack the tact!).

Once you acknowledge the elephant in the room, say something like:

Sometimes in life you and I get put into situations where clearly something is off, something is not right. And it's in those times that you and I must make a decision: Do we have the courage to say something, or do we remain silent and pretend like it isn't there?

Option 2: It's Hard to Say

To get them thinking about things that are hard to say, why not open with some good old-fashioned tongue twisters? Ask for a few volunteers who would like to compete to see who can say the following phrases five times in a row, quickly. See who can do it!

- She sells seashells by the seashore.
- Betty brought bitter butter, but Billy bought better butter.
- Which wristwatches are Swiss wristwatches?

Say something like:

Some things in life are hard to say because they are hard to pronounce. There are other things in life that are hard to say because they require us to be brutally honest with someone we love. Will we let the difficulty keep us from trying to share an important message, or will we go ahead, even when it is hard to say?

Prophet Profile: Nathan

- Most well-known for having the courage to call out a king (David) for his sin with Bathsheba.
- One of the few advisors in King David's cabinet who remained loyal throughout his entire reign.
- Later in life, he played a key role in making sure Solomon was the next king to sit on the throne of David.

A Prophet in Action

Standing in front of a King is not easy. We are used to a country where power is divided among a President, Senate, Congress, and Supreme Court. It is hard to imagine an era when one person could fulfill all those rules at the same time, but that is what the King did. With one word, a King could reward you with wealth and power or take away your life. When a King has that much power, it is hard to get up the nerve to talk to him.

Think About It:
Can you think of a time when you had to talk to someone, but you were dreading it? How did you feel?

As scary as it was, there was something serious that needed to be addressed, and there was only one person with the faith to do it. The King was determined to ignore the issue, but one man took it upon himself to make sure that didn't happen.

That man's name was David.

As a young man, he stood before King Saul and told him that Goliath, the Philistine giant who had been taunting the Israelites, needed to be defeated. No other soldier in Israel was willing to face off with Goliath, but David was. He was following a moral compass that was guided by his faith in God.

In one of the most well-known passages in Scripture, 1 Samuel 16 shows God giving David victory over the nine-foot-tall, experienced warrior. David was a hero. Israel was victorious. That was a great day.

But by 2 Samuel 11, much time has passed since that battle against Goliath. David is no longer that same young man. He is now older, sitting on the throne himself, as Israel's king. In fact, 2 Samuel 11:1 tells us that while other kings were out to battle, David stayed in Jerusalem.

Sharing the Prophets

The mighty warrior king who would not back down before foreign armies stood on his roof and surrendered to another enemy: temptation. He saw a beautiful woman taking a bath on her roof (I know that sounds strange to us, but it was not uncommon in a crowded city in the ancient world). He asks who she is, finds out she is married to one of his most faithful warriors, and sends for her anyway. Not too long after their night together, she discovers that she is pregnant.

Not only was the young giant-slayer now gone, it seems that his moral compass was gone too.

Here's another scary thing—even though David had done something wrong, it dawned on him that he had the power as a king to make it all go away. He invited her husband, a soldier named Uriah, back to Jerusalem from the battlefield. Maybe if Uriah spent some time at home, he would think the child was his.

When Uriah was too faithful to enjoy time at his house while his fellow soldiers were fighting, David had to go a step further: He arranged for Uriah to be on the front lines, and he told his commander Joab to back up the troops so that Uriah was guaranteed to die. After that happened, he sent for Bathsheba and married her.

Does this sound like the young man who stood before the King and talked about God's power?

Think About It:
Sometimes doing one wrong thing can lead to other wrong decisions. What are some examples of one bad decision leading to another?

In 2 Samuel 12, the prophet Nathan comes on the scene. It is obvious by this point that David has lost his sense of direction. He is ignoring the moral compass that had led him to victory in battle and instead is plotting his own course. Like someone determined to drive his car on his own route, no matter what the voice on the GPS says, David is ignoring clear guidelines from God.

Sharing the Prophets

Do not commit adultery, do not murder, do not lie. Weren't those three of the 10 commandments?

Nathan had a tough job: He had to convince the most powerful person in the kingdom to stop doing his own thing and listen to God. How would he do it? (Read vss.1-6 and vss.7-15.)

What happens next is unexpected—Nathan tells David a story. He describes two men who lived in a city. One was rich, with a great number of flocks and herds (a way to measure someone's wealth in the ancient world). The other had one little lamb that he raised and treated like a member of the family. The rich man was hosting a traveler at his home, and they would need meat for a meal. The rich man didn't feel like choosing from his own livestock, so he took the other man's only lamb.

By this point in the story, David is furious. As the King, he is used to making snap judgments on cases like this, and he blurts out, "The man who has done this deserves to die."

What happens next is not just unexpected, it is unheard of. The prophet Nathan stood before David and told the King, "You are the man." In other words, Nathan told the most powerful man in the nation that he deserved to die.

Gulp.

Think About It:
By telling this story, Nathan allowed David to get a true perspective on what he had done. What can Nathan's strategy teach us about how to discuss difficult situations with other people?

Nathan doesn't stop there, though. He gives David a message from God. God had provided David with everything, but even with all he had, David still chose to do evil. Since his sins resulted in the death of Uriah, David deserved to pay with his life. Yet, God took away his sins (2 Samuel 12:13).

You see, that is one thing the king of Israel could not do—forgive sins. Only the true King can do that.

Even though his sins were forgiven, there would still be consequences. David had told Nathan that the rich man in the story should pay the poor man back four-fold (four times what was required), and Nathan then told David there would be four consequences for his sin: (1) The sword would never depart from his house—there was more violence to come for David's family. (2) Evil would arise from David's own family—his own son, Absalom, would one day try to take the kingdom away from him. (3) David's wives would be taken by another—Absalom would later fulfill this prophecy as well, and (4) The child of David and Bathsheba would die.

Nathan took a stand, and he was willing to tell David the truth. Even when it was bad news. Even when it was unpleasant. Even when it was scary. Nathan's actions also teach us some important truths about the truth.

We need the truth, because we don't always see ourselves accurately.

David could clearly see what was wrong with a rich man who stole from a poor man, but he had managed to rationalize his own sins. Have you ever noticed that it is easier to find things wrong with other people than it is to see those same failures in our own lives?

We need the truth, because our sins affect other people.

When we think about sin, we often treat it as a personal issue between God and us. Sin is personal, but it impacts more than just the person who sins. Uriah lost his life because of David's sin. Bathsheba lost a husband and son because of David's sin. There would be more death and loss to come for David's family. Sin hurts me, but it hurts others as well.

We need the truth, because we need forgiveness.

If we read 2 Samuel 11 and 12, it looks like everything is going fine for David as he covers up his sin. But notice the words of Psalm 32. The heading connects this psalm of David with his emotions after covering up his what he had done, "When I kept silent about my sin, my body wasted away through my groaning all day long. For day and night Your hand was heavy upon me; my vitality failed as with the dry heat of summer" (v. 3-4, NASB). Covering up his sins hadn't made David's guilt go away, it made it worse. The only One that can make our sins go away and provide ultimate forgiveness is God, and we can't find His forgiveness until we are willing to accept the truth.

Think About It:

What are some consequences of sin that we don't often consider? How does reminding ourselves of those consequences affect our view of sin?

Looking to Jesus

In Deuteronomy 18:15, Moses referred to a prophet like him that would one day rise up and speak words commanded by God, and Jesus fulfills this role in the New Testament. In John 7:16, Jesus says, "My teaching is not mine, but his who sent me" (ESV). This is one of many passages where Jesus makes it clear He is sharing the message of the Father. Jesus is more than just a prophet. He is the Messiah, the Son of God. But we can see several characteristics of prophets whom Jesus displayed in His ministry.

One key trait of Jesus' ministry was that He told the truth to those who were in power. During Jesus' time on earth, one religious group called the Pharisees had a great deal of authority and religious power among the Jews. Yet Jesus was not afraid to tell them the Father's message.

Pharisees liked to give, pray, and fast in public so that others could see how spiritual they were. Yet Jesus said if they did that, earthly attention would be their only reward (Matthew 6:1-18). Pharisees would sometimes declare their money as reserved for God to avoid caring for aging parents (Mark 7:11-13). Jesus said those actions invalidated God's Word. Many Pharisees were concerned with the outward impression they made on others, but Jesus said that made them "whitewashed tombs" (Matthew 23:27). Jesus was not afraid to tell the truth.

One of the ways Jesus described Himself is "the Way, and the Truth, and the Life" (John 14:6). Jesus gives truth, always in love. In fact, the most loving thing we can do for anyone is tell them the truth. During another time when Jesus was telling people truth they didn't want to hear, He said, "The truth will set you free" (John 8:32). The truth does set us free, and we find the truth from Jesus.

Prophet Sharing

Do you have a friend right now who is headed down a dangerous path and needs your influence? How can you be a Nathan to that person?

Mystery Object: MATCH

What do you think Elijah has to do with a match?

Elijah had a match against the prophets of Baal, and he called down fire from heaven.

Ice Breakers

Option 1: Rock, Paper, Scissors
Get your students to partner up to play a quick game of Rock, Paper, Scissors (we don't really have to teach you how to play this game, do we?!?). This will go fast, so "best two out of three" would probably work best! They can face off against the person sitting next to them. The winners advance each time, until you reach the final two contestants. Hype it up. Have fun with it! And then clearly crown the champion. You could even award them with some sort of prize (candy for the win?).

Say something like:
That was a pretty epic showdown, but today we're going to look at an even bigger story about a high stakes showdown in God's Word. Turn with me to 1 Kings 18:20.

Option 2: Let's Make a Deal

Some game shows stand the test of time, and "Let's Make a Deal" is one of those that has been produced in many different countries and is still on every day in the U.S. (You might want to watch a clip online to check out the basic premise if you have never seen it).

Before class, come up with three goofy gifts (the sillier the better) and put each one behind a large piece of posterboard indicating either Door 1, 2, or 3. The gifts can range from things found around the church building to what you discover cleaning out your garage. The bottom line is that these "gifts" are inexpensive and not all that desirable.

Select a willing student to be your contestant, and begin to make a deal!

Ask the student to choose a door (you can even get the whole class involved in helping the contestant make these choices). Once that decision has been made, open one of the other doors to reveal a prize that was missed (hopefully students will laugh at that gift, and your contestant might get a little nervous about the selected door).

There will be two doors left; give your contestant the chance to either switch doors or stick with the original choice. Then, reveal what is behind the other door that was not chosen. As a last step, you could offer the contestant to trade what was behind the last door for a candy bar and see what happens. This way, a student goes home with something—either a candy bar or a crazy gift.

Say something like:

Some decisions in life are hard, because we don't know where a certain choice might lead. Some choices are simple, however, and today we are going to focus on a time when hundreds of people were challenged to make the clear choice of serving God. Turn with me to 1 Kings 18:20.

Prophet Profile: Elijah

- Name means, "My God is Yahweh."
- One of the most famous and beloved prophets.
- Elisha's mentor.
- The first person that we know of who raised someone from the dead (1 Kings 17:17-24)
- Some people apparently believed that Jesus was the second coming of Elijah! (Matthew 16:13-14)
- Appeared on the mountain of transfiguration with Jesus and Moses.
- Elijah never died! He was carried into heaven by a whirlwind (2 Kings 2:11).

Prophet in Action

Imagine you are preparing to make a presentation in front of your entire history class. You studied hard for it, but you're still nervous. Then your history teacher tells you that your entire grade will come to hear it. Your heart starts pounding, and then your principal walks up and suggests that you share your presentation with the entire school.

You may have spoken in front of hundreds of people before, but this would be a new experience for most people. Even if you are used to public speaking, making a presentation in front of that many people requires careful preparation.

Now imagine that all those people disagreed with what you had to say. How would you feel?

This is the situation in which Elijah found himself on Mount Carmel. He had to confront King Ahab, who had turned his back on God and started worshipping idols. Many nations in the area worshipped the god, Baal. Though that name was used for several different gods in other cultures, records indicate that Baal was often known as a weather god, the "rider on the storm." Israel had experienced a drought, so there were 450 prophets of Baal who were going to call on Baal to send rain. Elijah would face off with them as the only prophet of God, and they would see which one answered.

But that was not all Elijah would have to face. First Kings 18:19 tells us there were not only 450 prophets of Baal, but there were also 400 prophets of the goddess, Asherah, another popular pagan god. Imagine one man facing off against 850 other people who were completely against him.

Take a few minutes to read 1 Kings 18:20-39 to find out what happened.

Think about it:
Have you ever been with a group of people and realized that you are the only one there who believes in God. How does that feel?

Elijah starts off by asking them to make a choice: If the Lord was God, they should follow Him, but if they thought Baal was god, they should follow him. This sounds a lot like what Israel's leader from generations earlier said before they entered the Promised Land: "Choose this day whom you will serve, whether the gods your fathers served in region beyond the River, or the gods of the Amorites in whose land you dwell. But as for me and my house, we will serve the LORD" (Joshua 24:15). The choice for faithfulness always comes down to a decision between God and something else.

When I (Andrew) was growing up, we would always get to school early. My mother taught second grade, so while she went to her classroom, I would wait downstairs with the other students. We would bring baseball cards, basketball cards, and G.I. Joe action figures to trade. When a trade was proposed, we would examine each item as if we were inspecting a new car. We were serious about these trades. In fact, we are usually incredibly careful when we are trading something that seems valuable to us. When it comes to our relationship with God, do we ever "make trades" without thinking about it?

Think about it:
Can you think of any examples where someone might "make a trade" and choose not to stand up for God in favor of doing something else?

Elijah was not going to trade faithfulness to God for the approval of these prophets, and his example illustrates principles of faithfulness that are still important today.

God is with us, even when we feel outnumbered.

Elijah delivered his challenge. Since we don't live during a time of animal sacrifices, it might sound strange, but Elijah challenged them to bring two bulls to sacrifice on two separate altars. Elijah would pray to God, they would pray to Baal, and the One who sent down fire would be the one true God.

What happens next is intense. The prophets cry out to Baal for hours, even cutting themselves, but there was no answer. Finally, at noon, Elijah called the people near him, and built an altar with 12 stones (one for each tribe of Israel). He had them pour four jars of water on the offering and the wood, until water filled the trench surrounding the altar. When he called out to God, God sent down a fire strong enough to consume the offering, the wood, the stones, the dust, and even the water. There was no doubt who was in charge.

The next few sentences are hard to read, because they describe violent actions. We need to understand that conflicts between prophets, especially in the Old Testament, were not simply disagreements. The prophets of Baal were not only shown up, but they were also killed. Then God sent rain, and Elijah ran down to Jezreel. Put yourself in Elijah's place. How would you feel after all this happened?

God is with us, even when we feel alone.

Have you ever had a "spiritual mountaintop" experience, one of those times when you felt especially close to God and connected to your faith? What happened on Mt. Carmel would have been the ultimate spiritual mountaintop experience, and what we read in 1 Kings 19 shows us what we often encounter right after a mountaintop: a valley.

Think about it:

Share a time when you experienced a "spiritual mountaintop." How did it feel? Feeling can change quickly, so how can we remain faithful even we don't feel like we are on the mountaintop?

Jezebel, the queen, was not happy about what Elijah had done, and she sent word to Elijah that she was going to have him killed. He ran for his life, and even went a day's journey by himself into the wilderness. As he lay down under a juniper tree, he was exhausted, discouraged, and depressed. Have you ever felt like that?

On Mt. Carmel, Elijah stood up to hundreds of prophets. When Jezebel threatened him, he ran for his life. He went from feeling triumphant to being despondent. He was completely exhausted, and his servant had been sent away, which left him all alone. Sometimes our toughest spiritual moments can come after our greatest spiritual victories.

It is important to think about what happened in Elijah's life. He was physically exhausted. He had stood before a king, faced off with hundreds of prophets, run for his life, and walked a day into the wilderness. It is natural to feel down when we are physically exhausted. He sent away his servant, which left him alone. When we feel down, we are often tempted to withdraw from other people, but that is the time we need them the most. He was also being attacked by someone. When one person says or does something hurtful, it can be difficult to think about anything else.

Sharing the Prophets

Think about it:
Think of a time you were spiritually discouraged, and someone helped you get through it. What can we do to encourage our friends when they are struggling spiritually?

While in this difficult time, God provides for Elijah. He gave him food, and that food provided enough strength for Elijah to make it to Mount Horeb (otherwise known as Mount Sinai). This is the place where Moses received the 10 Commandments; 1 Kings 19:8 calls it the "mountain of God." Pause and read 1 Kings 19:9-19 to see what happened next.

Elijah was not alone. There were still 7,000 people who had not decided to worship Baal. Not only that, but God provided him with Elisha, an individual he would train to serve God as a prophet as well. Elijah had felt alone, but he wasn't. And neither are we.

Looking to Jesus

This is not the last time the voice of God will be heard on a mountain where Elijah is standing. Luke 9 tells us about a time Jesus took Peter, James, and John on a mountain to pray. The apostles had fallen asleep, and when they woke up, they were shocked by what they saw. Jesus had been transfigured, which means that His clothing was gleaming white, and even His face had become different. That would have been impressive enough, but Jesus was talking to two other people: Moses and Elijah.

Think about it:
Have you ever met one of your heroes? I don't know if it would be a certain athlete, a famous actor, or maybe a talented musician would be someone who would leave you star-struck, but just imagine standing across from that person. What would you say? Would you be able to say anything?

If you can imagine that feeling, you can picture how Peter, James, and John would have reacted when they saw two heroes of faith they had heard about for their entire lives. Moses, the one who led the Israelites out of Egypt, and Elijah, the powerful prophet. They were talking to Jesus about what was going to happen in Jerusalem. Jesus was going to be mistreated by powerful people who wanted to kill Him, and He would be abandoned by His friends. Doesn't that sound like a situation Elijah could understand?

Peter does exactly what we would do in the presence of heroes, he stammers out an idea he has not really deliberated. They could stay on the mountain and build three tents: one for Jesus, one for Moses, and one for Elijah. Then a cloud descended (something that often symbolizes God's presence in Scripture), and God said these words: "This is My Son, My Chosen One; listen to Him!" (Luke 9:35, NASB).

After that, Jesus was alone. The message was clear: Jesus is the Son of God, greater than the law (represented by Moses) and the prophets (represented by Elijah). The apostles would soon understand that although they had many heroes of faith, they would only have one Messiah.

Prophet Sharing

Consider Elijah's prayer in 1 Kings 18:36b-37:
> "O LORD, God of Abraham, Isaac, and Israel, let it be known this day that you are God in Israel, and that I am your servant, and that I have done all these things at your word. Answer me, O LORD, answer me, that this people may know that you, O Lord, are God, and that you have turned their hearts back" (ESV).

Sharing the Prophets

Notice what Elijah prays about here. Elijah's prays,

- Remembering who God is, the living, powerful God of Abraham, Isaac, and Israel. (vs.36)
- Remembering who he is, an obedient servant of God. (vs.36)
- Remembering that others need God. (vs.37)
- Expecting an answer. (vs.37)

Take the time right now to write a prayer like this. It doesn't have to be long, but in your prayer, (1) acknowledge who God is, (2) acknowledge who you are, (3) write down the name (or names) of someone who needs to know God, and (4) ask Him to answer the prayer.

Sharing the Prophets

Mystery Object: GLASSES

What do you think Elisha has to do with a pair of glasses?

Elisha had a godly perspective that allowed him to see situations from a spiritual point of view, the way God wants us to see things.

Ice Breakers

Option 1: The Awareness Test
You've probably seen this before, but this little video is a simple way to illustrate what can happen if we spend our time and attention focusing on the wrong things.

https://www.youtube.com/watch?v=Ahg6qcgoay4

After you show the video, say something like:
Isn't it crazy how much we fail to see, how much we miss, simply because we are looking at things in a different way? Sometimes it takes another set of eyes, another person (like a friend or a mentor), another perspective to help us see things that we might have missed at first glance. The truth is, we need people who will help us see from a godly perspective.

> "How does God view this?"
> "What would Jesus do in this situation?"
> "What does the Bible say about this idea?"

Elisha was a man who had a remarkable ability to see things from a godly perspective.

Option 2: Gehazeye (Gaaaze-eye?)

Remember Magic Eye from the '90s? There's a good chance nobody in your class does! This might be a great time to print off a few of those to bring to class and ask your students if they can see each image. You might want to print these on photo paper as the glare helps you see the images a little better. A simple Google image search will get you all the images you'll need.

Another option would be to use some of those classic optical illusions where you might see two faces or a vase, depending on how it looks at first to you. You can find a bunch of those here:

http://brainden.com/optical-illusions.htm

After you let them have fun with this concept for a few minutes, say something like:

Sometimes seeing pictures like these require us to look at something in a different way than we are used to, even in a deeper way. Sometimes we have to look beyond what first meets the eye and try to see things in a way that most people aren't used to seeing. Sometimes it takes another person (like a friend or a mentor) to help us see things that we might have missed at first glance. The truth is, we need people who will help us see from a godly perspective.

> *"How does God view this?"*
> *"What would Jesus do in this situation?"*
> *"What does the Bible say about this idea?"*

Elisha was a man who had a remarkable ability to see things from a godly perspective.

Sharing the Prophets

Prophet Profile: Elisha

- Because their names and stories are so similar, it can be tough to remember whether Elijah or Elisha came first. Just remember "J comes before S." If you can remember that Elijah's name comes first alphabetically, you can remember that Elijah's ministry came first, too.
- Was Elijah's understudy and successor.
- The miracles of Elisha were similar to Elijah's. Both Elijah and Elisha rolled back the rivers of the Jordan, both did miracles with jars of oil to provide for widows, and both raised widows' sons from the dead!
- Speaking of Elisha raising the widow's son from the dead, here's a weird fact: The Bible tells us that when the boy revived, he sneezed seven times (2 Kings 4:35).
- How's this for unique?!? Apparently, the dead body of Elisha still carried so much of God's power that when another dead man's body touched Elisha's bones, the dead man came back to life and stood up on his feet! (2 Kings 13:20-21)
- Interestingly, Elisha is only mentioned once in the New Testament. In Luke 4:27, Jesus uses the examples of Elijah and Elisha to illustrate how the Jews had been guilty of dishonoring prophets in their own hometowns. Elijah and Elisha would do great ministry for the Lord, but they would do it elsewhere. The Jews in Nazareth were about to make an even greater mistake by rejecting Jesus (in fact, in Luke 4 they are ready to throw him off of a cliff!), but that wouldn't keep him from doing great things for Lord either!

Prophet in Action

When someone extraordinary retires or steps down, people might say that person "left big shoes to fill." In 2 Kings 2, when Elijah is taken up to heaven and Elisha is left on earth, Elisha had big shoes (technically sandals) to fill. But God was with Elisha, just as He had been with Elijah. There are times we might be intimidated by something we have to do, but God can give us power to tackle those challenges.

One thing we notice early in life is that not everyone looks at things the same way. Both a doctor and her sick patient might look at an X-Ray, but the doctor will be searching for specific markers that the patient might not even notice. A biology professor might look through a microscope at the same specimen his student is studying, but only the professor can spot the features that will provide an accurate identification. One thing Scripture helps us do is view the world differently. If I am seeing things through the eyes of God, I will probably notice things other people miss. Though there were several incredible events in Elisha's life, two specific miracles help us understand the way Elisha saw the world. These two chapters will help us see the way God sees.

1. When I see the way God sees, I see the true Source of power.

Take a few minutes to read 2 Kings 5:1-14, and look for where the true power lies.

When we are introduced to Naaman, his resumé is impressive. He is an army commander who had won on the battlefield and had won over his master. There is one problem: He had leprosy.

The word *leprosy* in Scripture is a broad term that covers several different kinds of skin diseases. The law of Moses made sure that people with leprosy lived in separation from others, so that their family and friends would not be infected. But Naaman is not an Israelite, so he is carrying on with his life and career while searching for a cure.

Think about it:
Put yourself in Naaman's place. He had all the trappings of career success, but it wasn't enough. What does that tell us about what really matters in life?

That is when an Israelite servant girl mentions a prophet who could cure him, and Naaman listens. We can tell that Naaman is desperate, because Israel was not exactly an ally of Syria, yet Naaman was still willing to go there in search of relief. So Naaman goes straight to the top—the King of Israel. He shows up with a letter from the King of Syria asking that Naaman be cured of leprosy.

In Naaman's world of military order and armed conflict, power mattered. Therefore, he went to the most powerful person in Israel. Naaman did not understand that the power he was seeking would not be found in a palace.

The king of Israel wept, worried this might be some kind of trap. When Elisha discovers what has happened, he invites Naaman to come to his home. Naaman and his caravan of horses and chariots arrived at Elisha's home, and Elisha sent a messenger to Naaman. A messenger! Naaman was a commander. He didn't take orders from servants; he gave orders. Not only that, but why didn't Elisha come out himself? What could he possibly be doing that was more important?

Naaman didn't understand that the power to heal him wouldn't be found in a high-level meeting with a powerful figure, but in following simple instructions. In fact, there are two good decisions Naaman makes in this chapter:
1. To seek out Elisha
2. To obey Elisha's directions.

Sharing the Prophets

Both times, he followed the advice of lowly servants, not political leaders.

We often hear messages from celebrities or athletes that tell us how we should live, what products we should buy, and even how we should make our decisions. Yet sometimes the best advice comes from unexpected sources. What does this passage teach us about who we should listen to when it comes to making life decisions?

Let's pause for a minute and fast forward to 2 Kings 6. Read 2 Kings 6:11-19. Check out what this passage shows us about seeing as God sees.

By 2 Kings 6, the Syrians and the Israelites are at war, and the Syrians are frustrated that the prophet Elisha always seems to know their plans. When they find out that Elisha is in Dothan, they decide to go after him. This time, instead of seeing a caravan of chariots from an army commander outside his home, Elisha sees an army of horses and chariots surrounding his city. Understandably,

Elisha's servant sees the army and panics. He pleads with Elisha, asking, "What are we going to do?"

Elisha's response is powerful: "Those who are with us are more than those who are with them." He prays for his servant's eyes to be open, and they are. Then his servant can see the mountain full of horses and chariots of fire. God was in control, even when they couldn't see it. Elisha proves that by praying that God will strike the Syrian army with blindness, so that they could be led out of Dothan.

Seeing the way God sees requires us to open our eyes to the spiritual reality that He is in control. Paul uses that same imagery in Ephesians 1:18, praying that "the eyes of your heart" (NASB) will be enlightened, so that they could see the hope in Christ and the spiritual riches of their inheritance in Christ. In a world that can be discouraging, we must stop and open our eyes to God's power.

Think about it:
Can you think of a time you have felt overwhelmed by life and it seemed like you didn't know what to do? How can we pause during times like that and reflect on how God is with us?

2. When I see the way God sees, I see the importance of obedience.

Let's think back to Naaman again. Elisha gave him specific instructions to receive healing, but Naaman was not happy about it. He was supposed to go to the Jordan River and wash seven times for his skin to be clean. If you visit the Jordan River today, you will notice it is murky, not crystal clear. It seems like the same thing was true in Naaman's time, and he could think of several other rivers that were more appealing. By the time he thought about it, he was furious.

His servant asked him a good question, "If Elisha had asked you to do something great, wouldn't you have done it?" (2 Kings 5:13) In other words, Elisha's instructions were simple. Why wouldn't he do it? When he did obey, he received the healing that had been promised.

It seems like Elisha's instructions to wash in the Jordan River did not make sense to Naaman. Yet as soon as he did, he was healed. What does that teach us about obedience?

Naaman's leprosy went away, but it would come back before the chapter is over—just not to Naaman. Naaman was so moved by the healing, that he wanted to repay Elisha with presents. Elisha firmly refused, because money was not his primary concern. Once Naaman goes on his way, one of Elisha's servants named Gehazi has a different idea. He runs and catches up with Naaman, claiming that two young men had just shown up and Elisha needed some supplies (which was a lie). Naaman gladly gave him two talents of silver and two changes of clothes. Gehazi came back, hid what he had received, and tried to return to his usual routine.

Of course, he could not keep it secret for long. Elisha asked where he had gone, and Gehazi tried to act like he hadn't gone anywhere. Elisha saw through that lie, and he told Gehazi that it was not the right time to accept money. Because of Gehazi's dishonesty, Elisha tells Gehazi that he would receive leprosy, but not just any leprosy. The last verse of 2 Kings 5 reveals that the leprosy of Naaman clung to Gehazi for the rest of his life. This chapter begins and ends with leprosy. One is healed of it because of obedience, and one is given it because of disobedience.

Do you think Gehazi would have found it easy to rationalize the decision he had made to go behind Elisha's back? Can you think of some situations where it is tempting for us to rationalize when we make bad decisions?

Looking to Jesus

In 2 Kings 6, a servant's eyes are opened, and an army's eyes are blinded. In the Gospels, Jesus opens the eyes of several who are blind. One of those miracles took place in John 9, where Jesus and the apostles encountered a man who had been blind from birth.

Jesus chooses an interesting way to heal this man. He spits on the ground, making mud with His saliva, puts it in the man's eyes, and then instructs him to wash in the pool of Siloam. The man followed Jesus' instructions, and he came back seeing. He had the opportunity for healing, something he could never have provided on his own, but he had to obey Jesus to receive his sight.

Jesus also gives us the opportunity for something we could never provide for ourselves: salvation. Just like obedience was necessary for Naaman and for the man born blind, obedience is necessary for us. For example, the Book of Acts shows us how people become Christians, a process that always includes baptism. In Acts 2, Peter makes it clear that for us to receive forgiveness, we must repent and be baptized. Someone might ask why God commands us to be baptized, in the same way Naaman wondered why he needed to be washed in the Jordan River. Yet Scripture repeatedly reminds us that obedience is important, whether we completely understand the reasons behind a command or not. To receive the salvation Jesus has promised, obedience is necessary.

Prophet Sharing

It's easy for us to walk around and view our circumstances and situations entirely through a human point of view. But that isn't the way of God. Instead, he tells us to set our minds on things above, not upon things of the earth (Colossians 3:2).

What is a situation or a problem that you are facing right now that you need to see from a more godly perspective? What does God see when He looks at that situation? How can you be more like Jesus in dealing with this issue?

Sharing the Prophets

Isaiah: The Volunteer PROPHET

Mystery Object: EAR OF CORN AND A NEEDLE

Why is there an ear of corn and a needle? After you let them think on it for a minute, tell them: *"Corn has ears but cannot hear, and needles have eyes but cannot see. Later on Jesus would use this phrase to describe the Jews living in His day and time, but Jesus actually borrowed the phrase from Isaiah 6:9-10 where God tells Isaiah to say to the people, 'Keep on hearing, but do not understand; keep on seeing, but do not perceive.' Make the heart of this people dull, and their ears heavy, and blind their eyes; lest they see with their eyes, and hear with their ears, and understand with their hearts, and turn and be healed"*(ESV).

(Sorry for the corny illustration but needed to make a point. Get it? Needle…sorry.)

Ice Breakers

Option 1: Mad Gab®
Ever played Mad Gab®? It's really simple. Here's how it works. You hold up a piece of paper with words like this written on it.

Dishes Tea Vest Stay of Her

Sharing the Prophets

Usually, you play this game with two teams and at least two people on each team. One team member holds up the card with the strange words while their teammate tries to solve the phrase. (Be sure to write the answer on the back of the card so that the guesser can't see!) In the example above, the answer is, "This is the best day ever."

Others you can use:

1. **Cherry Hit Shove Hire** (chariots of fire)
2. **They've Hidden Bad Sheep Uh** (David and Bathsheba)
3. **Cher Ink The Prop Hits** (sharing the prophets)
4. **Go Hays Eye** (Gehazi)
5. **A Habit Chess A Pale** (Ahab and Jezebel)
6. **Hear Him Mice Enemy** (Here am I! Send me!)
7. **Eel Lied Ya Handy Lights Ya** (Elijah and Elisha)
8. **Oh Taste Um Improv Uh See** (Old Testament Prophecy)

When you're finished, say something like:

This game can be fun, but it can also be frustrating. You can see the words. You can heard the words. But you can still miss the message. Have you ever tried to communicate a message to someone, but no matter how much you tried, they just weren't getting it? That's frustrating, isn't it? I believe that's a feeling that the prophet Isaiah understood well. Turn in your Bibles to Isaiah 6.

Option 2: The Whisper Challenge

Jimmy Fallon, host of "The Tonight Show" on NBC does a game from time to time called "The Whisper Challenge" that should work pretty well for this illustration.

What You Need for this Game:

- A pair of noise canceling headphones (because every Bible class teacher owns a high-tech pair, right?)
- Two volunteers
- Clues written on index cards

Sharing the Prophets

How to Play:

One person wears the headphones and turns up the music so that they can't hear what the other person is saying. The other person picks up a card and reads the random phrase on the card. The person wearing the headphones has to guess what they just said. (Basically, the one wearing the headphones must read the other person's lips and correctly guess the phrase.)

Have your volunteers take turns after each clue. (Don't let it drag out too long! You might set a 20-second timer on each round.)

Here are some clues you could use (or feel free to make up your own).
1. Old MacDonald had a farm.
2. Viva Las Vegas
3. Batteries not included.
4. Didgeridoo
5. Follow the yellow brick road.
6. Batman and Robin

When you're finished, say something like:

This game reminds me of how frustrating it can be when we are trying to communicate with somebody about something, but no matter how hard we try to get them to understand, they just aren't getting it. That's frustrating, isn't it? I believe that's a feeling that the prophet Isaiah understood well. Turn in your Bibles to Isaiah 6.

Prophet Profile: Isaiah

- Name means "The LORD saves."
- Prophet in Judah before the time of Babylonian captivity. (Remember, God punished the kingdoms of Israel and Judah because of their unfaithfulness. God allowed Babylon to take Judah as their prisoners back to Babylon.)
- Ministered during the reigns of four different kings: Uzziah, Jotham, Ahaz, and Hezekiah.

- God told Isaiah to name one of his sons "Maher-shalal-hash-baz" (the longest name in the Bible), a phrase meaning "speed-spoil-hasten-plunder." The name represented the coming Assyrian invasion (8:1-4).
- God told Isaiah to walk around naked and barefoot for three years as a sign against Egypt and Cush! (Isaiah 20)
- According to Jewish history, Isaiah was sawed in half during the reign of Manasseh. If true, Hebrews 11:37 could be a reference to Isaiah's death.

Prophet in Action

The Book of Isaiah is one of prophecy, which means it is a collection of visions and prophecies God gave to Isaiah. Even though it isn't located at the beginning of the book, Isaiah 6 seems to describe Isaiah's calling as a prophet. He begins by stating that he saw this vision of God in the last year King Uzziah was in power. This provides a contrast between earthly kings and the Heavenly King.

Second Chronicles 26 tells us about Uzziah whose name means "strength." Uzziah came to power at age 16, and he developed a reputation as a powerful ruler. Eventually, his pride led to unfaithfulness—later on in Uzziah's story, God struck him with leprosy, which lasted until the day he died. He felt that he was strong, but God was stronger.

In Isaiah 6:1-13, Isaiah sees a contrast between this formerly mighty king with the truly powerful King.

The Messenger Will Always Be Imperfect.

When Isaiah sees the Lord on the throne, he is overwhelmed by an incredible scene. Not only is the throne lifted up, but the royal robe fills the entire temple. Verse 2 introduces us to Seraphim, angelic creatures with six wings that are praising God. The foundation of the room is trembling, and the room is filling with smoke. In the middle of all of this, Isaiah says something surprising, "Woe is me."

Sharing the Prophets

Since prophets give messages from God, they often had to share bad news. In Scripture, these negative messages often start with "Woe to..." In fact, the first five chapters of Isaiah contain eight different statements in which Isaiah pronounces "woes" on specific people, and seven of them are in chapter 5. If you want to read those "woes," check out Isaiah 3:9, 5:8, 11, 18-19, 20, 21, and 22-23. The "woes" in Isaiah are focused on sinners, those who were mistreating others, addicted to wine, and focused on their own wisdom.

Yet when he sees God, he pronounces a woe on himself. As he stands in front of the throne, he is reminded of his own shortcomings. God is going to ask for a spokesperson, but Isaiah knows he is a man of "unclean lips" from a nation of people with "unclean lips."

Whenever we look at God, we will always be reminded of our own failings. Yet an angel comes down with a hot coal to purify Isaiah's lips, which will give Isaiah the ability to share God's message. Even with all our sins, God can still use us to do His will.

Think about it:
How does understanding our own flaws affect the way we can share God's message?

Is it possible to be too open about our own faults when we talk to other people? What would be the consequences of being too open?

The Message Will Often Be Rejected.

After the coal has cleansed Isaiah's lips, he is able to speak, and his first words are, "Send me!" God had asked who would go out to represent God, and Isaiah's immediate response was to volunteer.

Have you ever volunteered (or "been volunteered" by someone else) for a job before you even knew what you would have to do? That is what Isaiah is doing here. He doesn't know what the message is going to be yet, but he is willing to step in and fill the role.

Sharing the Prophets

His job isn't going to be easy, though. God tells Isaiah, "Go, and say to this people: 'Keep on hearing, but do not understand; Keep on seeing, but do not perceive.'"

Take a minute to re-read that. He is telling Isaiah to preach to people, knowing that those people are not going to really listen. Have you ever tried to talk to someone who isn't listening to you? It is frustrating; when we communicate, we want to be heard. Not only that, but Isaiah is called to speak to Judah, God's people. His prophecies aren't going to be delivered to other nations, who we might expect to misunderstand what Isaiah is saying. He is going to preach God's message to God's people, and they will still misunderstand him.

Sometimes we associate the success of an idea with the number of people who believe it.

If everybody at school thinks a certain style of clothing looks good, then it must look good. If my friends all think a certain band is good, then it must be. In this passage, we are reminded that God's message will not always be popular; in fact, it will often be unpopular.

Just because there are a lot of people in the world who do not believe in God, that doesn't mean His message is wrong. It just means that we are facing a challenge that has always existed for followers of God: Not everyone will believe what we believe. Our challenge is whether we will stand firm on what we believe, no matter what.

Why do you think there are many people in our culture who have heard about God but have chosen not to believe? What should we remember in our conversations with them?

God Will Never Be Defeated.

The chapter does not end on a completely negative note, though. Isaiah is going to have to preach difficult messages to Judah, and he will have to tell them about their impending captivity in Babylon.

Sharing the Prophets

But even after the Babylonians take God's people captive, verse 13 tells Isaiah that there will be a few left (a "tenth remain" in verse 13). This is something that happens a lot when we read prophecy: There is a difficult message, but it concludes with a reminder of God's mercy and hope for the future. No matter how defeated Judah may feel, they needed to remember that this captivity would not be the end of God's people or His plan.

After all, Isaiah served the truly powerful Ruler, the one on the throne. That is the Ruler we serve as well.

Looking to Jesus

If you read through the Gospel of Matthew, you will find several references to Isaiah. It seems that

Matthew was originally written primarily to a Jewish audience, to show them that Jesus was the Messiah, and because of that, Matthew refers often to Isaiah's prophecy. One of those references comes after a famous parable, the parable of the Sower in Matthew 13. To read the entire parable, check out Matthew 13:1-9.

We usually think of parables as stories that take a difficult concept and put it in language everyone can understand. There were times, though, when parables could be confusing. Parables could function like riddles, offering meaning only after listeners had put in serious mental work. His apostles asked Jesus why He taught this way. Jesus responded by comparing many of His hearers to Isaiah's audience.

He quotes Isaiah 6:9-10, saying that many of his listeners were seeing without perceiving and hearing without understanding. Even Jesus faced the challenge of speaking to those who didn't (and often wouldn't) understand. When that happens to us, we can know it happened to Him, too.

Prophet Sharing

In the year that King Uzziah died I saw the Lord sitting upon a throne, high and lifted up; and the train of his robe filled the temple. Above him stood the seraphim. Each had six wings: with two he covered his face, and with two he covered his feet, and with two he flew. And one called to another and said: "Holy, holy, holy is the LORD of hosts; the whole earth is full of his glory!" And the foundations of the thresholds shook at the voice of him who called, and the house was filled with smoke. And I said: "Woe is me! For I am lost; for I am a man of unclean lips, and I dwell in the midst of a people of unclean lips; for my eyes have seen the King, the LORD of hosts!" Then one of the seraphim flew to me, having in his hand a burning coal that he had taken with tongs from the altar. And he touched my mouth and said: "Behold, this has touched your lips; your guilt is taken away, and your sin atoned for." And I heard the voice of the Lord saying, "Whom shall I send, and who will go for us?" Then I said, "Here I am! Send me." (Isaiah 6:1-8)

Look back at the passage above about Isaiah being in the presence of the LORD. What responses do you see Isaiah having to this experience (vss.5-8)?

Notice the progression: unworthy and sinful (vs.5), forgiven and atoned for (vss.6-7), responsible and eager to serve (vs.8).

How should our response to God be similar to Isaiah's?

Who might God be sending you to go and reach? Pray for an opportunity to reach them this week.

Jeremiah: The Weeping PROPHET

Mystery Object: TISSUES

This one might be on the easier side: Does anyone have any guesses about why tissues represent Jeremiah?

Jeremiah is often referred to as the weeping prophet because of the many tears he shed during times of great difficulty in his ministry.

Ice Breakers

Option 1: Minute-to-Win-It Tissue Box

This one is a lot easier to prep, especially if you brought the mystery item to class. Basically, you do the classic "Minute-to-Win-It" challenge in which the contestant has one minute to pull all the tissues out of a tissue box using only one hand.

Want to mix things up a little bit more (personally, I think that the "Minute to Win It" version of the game is too easy)? Get two tissue boxes and let two students race to see who can do it first.

Still not good enough for you?!? Set the game on hard mode by having the contestants complete this challenge using only their mouths.

What they win is up to you!

As for a segue into the lesson, just go ahead and reveal why the mystery item is a box of tissues (because you are studying Jeremiah the weeping prophet!).

Sharing the Prophets

Option 2: Play-Doh® Pictionary®

Basically, you are going to play Pictionary with Play-Doh.

Divide your class into two teams, and make sure you have at least two containers of Play-Doh (more is okay, and it would probably help them to have some different color options!). Teams need to choose one person from their team to sculpt the clue while the rest of the team shouts out guesses. The first team to answer correctly gets the point. After each clue, be sure to change "sculpters" so that everybody (or as many as time will allow) gets a turn. And of course, crown the winner however you'd like.

Here are a few Play-Doh Pictionary clue ideas, but feel free to use your own!

- Elephant
- Cowboy
- Coffee mug
- Football helmet
- Stapler
- Computer
- Waterslide
- Backpack
- Picture frame
- Preacher

After the activity, say something like:

I thought this would be a great way to begin our study on Jeremiah this morning, because one of most famous things about him is about a visit that God tells him to make at the house of a potter (someone who sculpts things out of clay). We'll talk more about that in a minute, but here are some other things you may or may not know about Jeremiah...

Prophet Profile: Jeremiah

- Lived during the reign of five kings of Judah.
- Spent his days warning the nation of Judah about God's coming judgment for their wickedness.
- Eventually saw the city of Jerusalem destroyed and the nation overtaken by Babylon.

Sharing the Prophets

- The meaning of his name is uncertain. Possibilities include "The Lord exalts" or "The Lord establishes," while another could be "The Lord throws," either in the sense of Jeremiah being thrown into a hostile environment or of how the Lord would throw down the nations in divine judgment.
- Commanded by God not to marry and have children because they would be killed in the coming devastation and judgment of Judah (16:1-4).
- Closest companion was his secretary, Baruch, who recorded the words that Jeremiah would speak.
- Ministry marked by persecution, stress, and unhappy messages of doom and judgment. Even still, all hope was not lost: Jeremiah also spoke of God's mercy, forgiveness, of Jesus (the righteous Branch in 23:5-6; 33:14-16) the New Covenant (31:31-34), and of God's plans to restore those who had been taken to Babylon (29-31).
- People hated Jeremiah and conspired to harm (and even kill him) on many occasions—he was mocked, beaten, imprisoned, put in stocks, left to starve inside a mud-filled cistern, and according to Jewish tradition, was ultimately put to death by being stoned (would fit with Hebrews 11:37).
- Famously said, "If I say, 'I will not mention him, or speak any more in his name,' there is in my heart as it were a burning fire shut up in my bones, and I am weary with holding it in, and I cannot" (20:9)
- Also penned, "The steadfast love of the LORD never ceases. His mercies never come to an end; great is our faithfulness. 'The LORD is my portion,' says my soul, therefore I will hope in him" (Lamentations 3:22-24).
- God used several unique images to communicate His messages to and through Jeremiah.
- Vision of a boiling pot being overturned from the North represented how God's wrath was going to be poured out upon Judah through His vessel, Babylon. (1:12-19)

Sharing the Prophets

- Buried a spoiled, good-for-nothing pair of underwear (for real) to represent how God would spoil the pride of Judah, and to show how their wicked, idolatrous ways were good for nothing. (13:1-11)
- Observed a potter shaping clay to illustrate how God would shape disaster against Judah. (Jeremiah 18)
- Broke a flask of pottery to illustrate how God would break and punish Jerusalem. (Jeremiah 19)
- Had a vision of good figs and bad figs—good figs representing the good God planned for the exiles He would bring back, and bad figs representing the wickedness left in Judah and the punishment God would bring upon them (Jeremiah 24).
- Sent by God on a trip to many nations with a cup of wine (representing God's cup of wrath) and told to make the officials of the nations drink it, saying, "They shall drink and stagger and be crazed because of the sword that I am sending among them" (25:16).
  - Made and wore a wooden yoke and speak to the people, illustrating that the nation would be under the yoke of Babylon (Jeremiah 27). When a false prophet didn't like what he had to say and took the wooden yoke from him and broke it, the LORD informed the people that their yoke had would be upgraded to a yoke of iron! (28:10-17)
- Purchased a field in a city (Jerusalem) that was in the process of being destroyed (certainly a strange time to buy real estate). However, as God explained to Jeremiah, this was to show His long-term plan to make what was once desolate in Jerusalem prosper again: the fields, the city, and even the economy (Jeremiah 32).

Prophet in Action

It happens a lot, and it is always awkward. Someone asks you to go see a movie you don't want to see, or your friend asks you to come over when you are so tired that you just want to go home and go to sleep. You have been asked to do something you don't want to do, and now you have to decide how to react. You start racking your brain to come up with a reason to say no.

Think about it:
What is the best excuse you have ever come up with to avoid something you didn't want to do?

But what if the request was for more than just a two-hour movie or an afternoon hanging out with someone? What if you were asked to accept a mission that would consume your entire life? That is what happened with Jeremiah. In Jeremiah 1, we see exactly how he received his call to be a prophet. If these verses sound familiar, it is because we see more than one person in Scripture make excuses when God calls for a major mission (like Moses and Gideon, for example).

Read Jeremiah 1:1-10 to see what happens when Jeremiah is called by God to be a prophet. As you read this, ponder this question: How was God going to use Jeremiah?

God saw something in Jeremiah.
Have you ever had someone see something in you that you couldn't see in yourself? Maybe your coach put enough confidence in you to make you a starter when you weren't sure you could do it. Maybe a teacher asked you to help someone who was struggling with schoolwork, even though you had never thought of yourself as a tutor.

It is a good feeling when someone has confidence in you, but it can be scary. That is the way Jeremiah feels in chapter 1. In Jeremiah 1,

Sharing the Prophets

God revealed that He had a purpose for Jeremiah, even before he was born, but Jeremiah starts searching for an excuse. He basically tells God, "I am too young—I won't know what to say!"

Have you ever been too young to do something? Because of my birthday, I (Andrew) was always the youngest in my class. I was the last person in my class to get my driver's license, and I couldn't wait to be old enough to drive on my own. But as soon as I got behind the wheel on my own, with my new driver's license in my wallet, I felt young and inexperienced. It took a while for me to feel like I belonged on the road.

When Jeremiah hears this responsibility, that he is going to stand before God's people and prophesy, he immediately feels too young. How would he know what to say? What if people didn't listen?

Think about it:
Have you ever thought you were too young or inexperienced to do something? How did it feel?

When we are little children, we are in a hurry to grow up. We want to be tall enough to ride the big rides at the fair, and we want to be old enough for our parents to trust us to stay home by ourselves. We might feel like our age limits us, but the Bible is filled with young people who do incredible things. Daniel is described as a "youth" (Daniel 1:4) when he makes up his mind to stand up for God in Babylon. Josiah began his reign as King of Judah at a young age, and he was still a "youth" when he began to follow God and lead the people in the right direction (2 Chronicles 34:3). That is why Paul would tell Timothy, "Let no one despise you for your youth, but set the believers an example in speech, in conduct, in love, in faith, in purity" (1 Timothy 4:12).

Think about it:
We don't have to wait until we are a certain age to serve God. Take a few minutes to brainstorm at least seven ways you can serve God right now.

Sharing the Prophets

Jeremiah had his doubts. He initially resisted the way God wanted to use him. He would learn later that God can choose to use us in whatever way He thinks is best.

In Jeremiah 18, God sends him to the potter's house, where he watches a potter molding a clay vessel on his potter's wheel. If you have ever watched someone use a potter's wheel, you have probably seen what Jeremiah 18:4 describes. The jar he was making was spoiled, so the potter smashed the clay back together again and started making a new vessel. God's message was for Israel, that He could choose to use them in whatever way He wanted, but it is also a reminder to us that God is the potter. Just like a clay pot wouldn't say to the potter, "Don't use me this way," we shouldn't say the same thing to God. He is the potter; we are the clay.

It is easy to play the comparison game. I look at myself in the mirror, and I wonder why I don't have the abilities of someone else I admire. Why can't I be as good an athlete as she is? Why doesn't school come as easily to me as it does to him? We can do the same with spiritual comparisons. Why can't I lead a song the way he can? Why don't I have the same ability to connect with other people that she does?

At times like this, we can remind ourselves that God is the potter and we are the clay; He chooses how to use us. He has equipped us with the abilities we have, and I need to think carefully about how I can use what He has given me to serve Him.

God planned something for Jeremiah.

God had a clear response when Jeremiah tried the "I'm too young" excuse. God told Jeremiah not to be afraid of those who would look down on him, because God would be with him. By the way, God said the same thing when Moses didn't think he was good enough to lead the people out of Israel. God told Moses, "I will be with you" (Exodus 4:12). When Gideon told God that he couldn't lead soldiers because he came from a small family, from a small tribe, God said, "I will be with you…" (Judges 6:16). Even when you feel like you aren't good enough or experienced enough to serve God, remember that He is with you.

Think about it:
Can you think of a time in your life when it was important for you to remember that God was with you?

Jeremiah's life as a prophet was not a recent idea; God planned it even before Jeremiah was born. God tells Jeremiah, "Before I formed you in the womb, I knew you." Just like God knows the number of hairs on our head (Matthew 10:30), He knew Jeremiah even before he was born. Think about that for a minute—God knows everyone better than they know themselves!

Think about it:
How does it make you feel to know that God knows you better than you know yourself?

Just like God had a plan for Jeremiah, God had a plan for his people. One of the most famous passages in Jeremiah is Jeremiah 29:11, taken from a letter written to the exiles in Babylon, where God tells them that even though things look bleak, He is still with them: "For I know the plans I have for you," declares the LORD, "plans for welfare and not for evil, to give you a future and a hope."

God gave something to Jeremiah.

Not only was God going to be with Jeremiah, He also gave Jeremiah His message. The Lord stretches out His hand, touches His mouth, and says, "I have put My words in your mouth" (Jeremiah 1:9).

Jeremiah did not have a powerful position or influence, but God stated that His message would be able to "pluck up and to break down, to destroy and to overthrow, to build and to plant" (Jeremiah 1:10). That is a phrase that shows up more than once in Jeremiah, and it reminds us that even though there were leaders who thought they were powerful, they could not overpower God's word.

In fact, God's word was more powerful than Jeremiah himself. Later, in Jeremiah 20:9, Jeremiah would say, "If I say, 'I will not mention him, or speak any more in his name,' there is in my heart as it were a burning fire shut up in my bones, and I am weary with holding it in, and I cannot." Even if he tried not to say anything, he couldn't help sharing what God had given him.

Here is why it's important for us remember this: Jeremiah's life was not an easy one. He had a hard time getting people to listen, and they responded with threats, mocking, physical persecution, and even imprisonment. Even though Jeremiah warned against Judah being taken captive, it still happened. Success is not determined in the short term. God would be victorious even after the nations in power had faded from the earth.

The same is true today. Sometimes it feels like we are the only ones who believe what the Bible says. We think we are the only ones trying to do what is right or trying to live the way God wants us to live. Even when we feel completely alone, we can look at the life of Jeremiah and realize that these circumstances are not permanent.

No matter how long it takes, God will be victorious.

Looking to Jesus

When we read the New Testament, we find out that just as God saw something in Jeremiah, He sees something in us. When Jesus describes His mission in John 3, He tells us He came so that the world (all of us) might be saved. Every human being is made in the image of God (Genesis 5:2). Every one of us represents a soul Jesus died to save.

God sees something in us.

Not only does God see something in us, but He also had a plan for us, before any of us were born. In Ephesians 1:4, Paul tells us that God had a plan for the church "before the foundation of the world." It has always been God's plan that everyone in the world would have the opportunity to become part of His church.

God planned something for us.

Just as God gave Jeremiah His word, God has given us His word as well. God's Word is so powerful that it prepares us for everything we need—to know how to become a Christian, to get to know God, and to learn how to live. Here's how 2 Timothy 3:16-17 describes God's Word: "All Scripture is breathed out by God and profitable for teaching, for reproof, for correction, and for training in righteousness, that the man of God may be complete, equipped for every good work."

God gave something to us.

Prophet Sharing

Just as God warned his people in the Old Testament, He has warned us, too, of a coming day of judgment, and even though Jeremiah's audience might've ignored God's warning, we cannot afford to make that mistake.

The good news is there is something we can do about it: We can be saved through Jesus.

What about you? Is it time for you to turn from sin and surrender yourself to God?

What are you waiting for?

Ezekiel: The "PROP-PHET"

Mystery Object: BONES (or A SKELETON)

Ezekiel is most well-known for his vision of a valley filled with dry bones.

Ice Breakers

Option 1: Prop a See
This one should be fun.

Bring a black trash bag filled with random items (think "Skit Bags" if that helps!). Have your students pair up (or pair them up yourself), and then have each team reach inside the bag without looking and pull out one item.

Tell them their job is to figure out how they would use that object in a Bible lesson. (For example, a team might randomly select a flowerpot. They could make a lesson about how to grow in your faith or about having a faith that takes root, etc.)

Give them two to three minutes to prepare, and then let them make a short presentation in front of the class. (Tip: Don't take too long on this! If you have a large class, consider letting them work in groups.

Say something like:
Today, we're going to be studying one of the most unusual prophets you'll ever read about. His name was Ezekiel, and he was pretty much the king of random illustrations.

Option 2: Bone or No Bone?

Supplies needed:
- Pens
- Paper
- Candy as a reward

This one is really simple, but I think you'll like it.

Say something like:
"We're going to play a game called 'Bone or No Bone.' Here's how it works. I will read you a word and a definition. All you have to decide is whether the word is a bone in your body or not. It should be pretty simple. Oh, and no phones on this quiz (that's cheating). At the end, you guys can grade your own papers and see how you did. (And of course, the winner gets candy!)

Flaval bone: mostly found in reptiles, this figure-eight shaped bone helps protect brain tissue. *(Not a bone)*

Vomer: one of the unpaired facial bones of the skull. *(Bone)*

Cubone: a term used to describe developing bone matter in the embryonic stage. *(Not a bone...in fact, it's a Pokemon.)*

Hyoid: a horseshoe-shaped bone situated in the anterior midline of the neck between the chin and the thyroid cartilage. *(Bone)*

Braechtune (pronounced "brock-tune"): a small bone located above the spine that plays a vital role in basic functions such as swallowing and breathing. *(Not a bone)*

Sacrum: a large, triangular bone at the base of the spine that forms by the fusing of sacral vertebrae between 18 and 30 years of age. *(Bone)*

Say something like:
Today we are talking about a prophet who is probably most well-known for a story about bones. His name is Ezekiel.

Prophet Profile: Ezekiel

- Called to be a prophet after being carried into Babylonian captivity (1:1-3)
- Told to eat a scroll in chapter 2-3, representing how the Lord would put his words in Ezekiel's mouth. The taste of the scroll was sweet like honey.
- In chapter 4, he was called to build what sounds like a toy model of a city under siege (I know it isn't the same, but I picture a play set assembled from a popular line of colored, interlocking plastic blocks) and to lie on his left side for 390 days and his right side for 40 days. The days represented years of punishment for the two nations. During that time, God told Ezekiel to cook his food in their sight on human dung but changes his mind and lets him use cow dung instead.
- In chapter 5, he was called to cut his beard and hair and use them to illustrate a prophecy.
- In chapters 6 and 36, he was called to prophesy to mountains.
- In chapter 12, he was told to pack his bags, dig through a wall, and leave town like an exile in the evening. Also, he was told to cover his face, symbolizing how the king of Judah would not be able to see the land to which he was going.
- Also in chapter 12, was told to tremble and anxiously eat a meal, symbolizing the way that the people of Judah would eat their food in dismay, since the city and the people were about to be destroyed.
- Riddle me this: In chapter 17, God tells Ezekiel to tell Israel a riddle.
- Told that the delight of his eyes, his wife, would be taken from him just as the temple, the delight of Israel's eyes, would be taken from her. Ezekiel was commanded not to mourn openly for his wife, as a sign that the people should not mourn openly for Jerusalem (24:15–27).

- In chapter 37, he was given a vision of a valley filled with dry bones. When he was told to speak to them, the bones rattled and joined together, forming bodies, and then grew flesh, like a zombie army. After that, the LORD brought the bodies back to life, symbolizing how God would bring His spiritually dead, broken people back to life (37:1-14).
- Told to take two sticks and write "For Judah" on one and "For Joseph" on the other, and then join the sticks together, symbolizing how God would join His people back to Him, uniting them under Jesus, the coming King and Good Shepherd (37:15-28).
- In chapter 38, he was told to prophesy to the animals! The birds of the air and the beasts of the field were told that God was preparing for them a sacrificial feast—an all-you-can eat buffet… of dead bodies. When God's judgment would be poured out against Israel, the animals fill themselves with the carcasses of the slain (39:17-20).

Prophet in Action

Most people don't typically like to spend a lot of time in a cemetery. We might go to visit the grave of someone we love, but chances are, we don't like to stay long. Cemeteries remind us that we won't live forever, which makes it a surprise that one of the most memorable moments in Ezekiel's life comes in a valley of bones. It isn't technically a cemetery, since the bodies are not buried, but it is a scene filled with dry bones.

Read Ezekiel 37:1-14, and try to imagine this scene.

What would God be trying to teach Ezekiel in a place like this?

Life Seemed Hopeless
Before Ezekiel found himself in a valley full of bones, he had already found himself in captivity.

Sharing the Prophets

Chapter 1 tells us that he had been carried off from Judah to Babylon. This took place when he was 30 years old, the age when priests usually began their service. He was entering that phase of his life in a place far different than the one he would have imagined. The Babylonians liked to take the nations they conquered and try to assimilate them, making them true Babylonians. It would have taken strength and determination to hold onto faith in God during that time.

Think about it:
Can you think of a time in your life where you felt lost or hopeless? What helped you get through those tough days?

In chapter 37, God set Ezekiel down in the middle of a large valley full of bones. The number of bones may suggest that a large battle had been fought there, and since the bones were dry, they had been there a while. That would be a scary place for any of us to land, but it would have been especially tough for Ezekiel, who was a priest. Touching a dead body would have made him unclean. He was in captivity, he was in a valley of dry bones, and then he was given a strange job.

Now, Ezekiel had already been given a lot of strange jobs in his ministry. He had been told to eat a scroll, to lie on his side for hundreds of days, and to prophesy to the mountains, but this one would be the most dramatic yet. He is told the prophesy to the dry bones. That's right—prophesy to the bones. These bodies died a long time ago, and bones don't have ears. The task seemed hopeless.

Hopelessness is heartbreaking, and it is a feeling that followers of God know well. Abraham was 100 years old, and his wife Sarah was 90, when they were promised a son by God. They looked at their lives and asked, "Can these bones live?" Gideon looked at the few men he had left to fight a battle and asked, "Can these bones live?" Nehemiah arrived in Jerusalem when the city was in terrible condition, and he wanted to rebuild it. He had to look at the ruins and ask, "Can these bones live?"

Think about it:
Take a few minutes to think of a few miracles included in Scripture. Which ones do you think would have caused the most amazement if you had seen them in person?

Maybe your family hasn't set a great example for you. Maybe home is a place filled daily with conflict, arguing, and fighting. Maybe you are dealing with the loss of someone you love, a person who was close to you. Maybe you have been wanting to share your faith with someone, but that person is completely uninterested.

When you are surrounded by hopelessness, you might wonder, *Will things ever get better? Will life ever feel normal again?* When you feel that way, you are essentially asking, "Can these bones live?"

Nothing Is Hopeless with God
In the middle of a hopeless scene, God performs an incredible miracle. When Ezekiel repeats God's message over the bones, they came together, the sinews connected them, and flesh covered them. God brought these dead bodies back to life.

Although this situation is amazing, it shouldn't be surprising. The God who was guiding Ezekiel was the God over all life.

God describes Himself this way in Deuteronomy 32:39—"It is I who put to death and give life" (NASB). This is evident from the creation of mankind in Genesis 2:7, "Then the LORD God formed man of dust from the ground and breathed into his nostrils the breath of life, and the man became a living creature."

God is the author of life. No matter what technological advances we develop, nothing can compare with His power.

Hopelessness is heartbreaking, but God's power is comforting. Abraham and Sarah's situation seemed hopeless, until God gave them Isaac. Gideon's army seemed hopeless until God gave him victory. The ruins of Jerusalem appeared hopeless when Nehemiah rode through it, until God enabled them to rebuild.

Sharing the Prophets

Hopelessness cannot overpower the Author of life.

It is important to notice when God's power was most clearly seen in the valley—when Ezekiel obeyed. In 37:7 and 10, Ezekiel says that he prophesied as he was commanded. The miracle happened because of God's power, but it happened when God's word was obeyed. In fact, throughout the Bible we are reminded that God is at work when we keep His Word. Several Old Testament psalms confirm the fact that God's Word is the only trustworthy guide for our lives. For instance, Psalm 119:9-10 puts it this way: "How can a young man keep his way pure? By guarding it according to your word. With my whole heart I seek you; let me not wander from your commandments!" The same concept is repeated in the New Testament, in places like James 1:25—"But the one who looks into the perfect law, the law of liberty, and perseveres, being no hearer who forgets but a doer who acts, he will be blessed in his doing."

Think about it:
Take a few minutes to think about some of the commands in Scripture. Can you think of some of those directions from God that would make the world better if everyone lived by them? Share them with your group.

Do we really believe God can change a hopeless situation? Do we really think that following God's Word will allow us to see His power in our lives? Ezekiel reminds us that our answer to those questions should be *yes*.

Sarah Andrews[1] was born in 1892. When she became an adult, she decided to follow a dream that had been planted in her heart by stories of missionaries and her desire to serve God. There were a couple of missionaries in Japan who needed help working with children and orphans. On Christmas Day, she said goodbye to her parents and moved to Okitsu, Japan. She spent 45 years in that Buddhist village, mastering the language and starting a Sunday School to minister to the children there. By 1919, there

---

[1] To learn more about Sarah's story, check out *Virtuous Servant* by Fiona Soltes.

were 100 children in her class, and by 1923, 170 children were going to that class. She even stayed there during World War II. After the war was over, lack of food in the area caused her to become seriously ill, down to 85 pounds. She was nursed back to health, and she helped rebuild Okitusu and resumed her Sunday School class. The children she taught began to grow up, become Christians, and serve God. The end result of her work is that four congregations were planted in Japan.

She entered a village that looked hopeless, and she stayed there through times that seemed hopeless. Yet she trusted in God to work through her efforts, and He did. He will do that for us, too, when we live for Him.

Looking to Jesus

Let's face it; Ezekiel had to do several things that did not make much sense. Preaching to a valley of bones definitely falls into that category. But when he did it, God was at work.

In the same way, Jesus often said things that didn't make much sense to the people around Him. In a world where Jews hated the Romans, who were in charge of them, Jesus told people to go the extra mile for a Roman soldier (Matthew 5:41). Even though our enemies can make us so furious that we want to lash out, Jesus told people to pray for their enemies (Matthew 5:44). The culture around us values money highly, but Jesus challenged people to realize serving God was more important than all our possessions (Luke 18:18-25).

Jesus also shows us that even though those statements might not seem to make sense, God is at work when we follow them. Many times, serving others can show them a godly example that might stick with them. Praying for people who hurt us can help us overcome resentment, and investing our time in serving God is more valuable than any money we could ever acquire. Because we serve a God who sees further than we can see, we can trust Him, even when things don't make sense.

Prophet Sharing

What is something that you can do for someone else that would be so kind and loving that it would confuse them? Maybe it's writing a letter to a teacher at school that most people don't like, giving a "thank you" note to a lunch lady, or buying the person's meal behind you in a drive thru. Be creative and come up with your own way of showing people a confusing, eye-catching, unmistakable, selfless kind of love: the love of Christ.

Sharing the Prophets

Daniel: The Almost Prey, Always Praying PROPHET

Mystery Object: LION

This one's a no brainer, I suppose, but you will need to find a stuffed lion to put inside a box. If you can't find a stuffed lion, a real one will also work. Just kidding!

Ice Breakers

Option 1: High Stakes Operation

Few things put as much pressure on a human being than the game "Operation®." Here's a great twist on a classic. You'll need to do a little prep, but this could be fun and it shouldn't take too long! You'll need…

Prep
- Operation® (the board game)
- A carton of one dozen eggs. Eleven of them need to be hardboiled but BE SURE NOT TO HARD BOIL ONE OF THE EGGS!
- Some sort of prize for the winner of this game (candy always works!)

Sharing the Prophets

What to Do
Choose two victims, I mean volunteers, who will face off in a high-stakes version of Operation. If one of the contestants buzzes Sam (that's the guy's name in Operation) on their turn, their turn is over and they must immediately choose and crack an egg over their forehead.

If they choose the egg that has not been hardboiled, it will of course explode and everybody (else) will laugh.

After the activity say something like:
How do you respond to pressure? When things around you get tense, what do you do? How do you handle high pressure situations?

Today we're going to be looking at a prophet who often found himself in the middle of many high-pressure, high-stress situations. But what's awesome about this guy is that pressure and stress didn't seem to change anything about who he was or how he acted. In fact, what we learn about him is that his faith prepared him for those high-pressure situations. His name is Daniel.

Option 2: Canned, But Not Crushed
This is an illustration I borrowed from a friend of mine, Wayne Miller (who borrowed it from someone else; I'm sure!). You'll need two aluminum cans: one that is completely empty and one that has not yet been opened.

Have your students turn to 2 Corinthians 4:7-10 and read it.
> *But we have this treasure in jars of clay, to show that the surpassing power belongs to God and not to us. We are afflicted in every way, but not crushed; perplexed, but not driven to despair; persecuted, but not forsaken; struck down, but not destroyed; always carrying in the body the death of Jesus, so that the life of Jesus may also be manifested in our bodies (2 Corinthians 4:7-10).*

Sharing the Prophets

Say something like:

Hold up the unopened aluminum can and talk about how sometimes as Christians we can go through some really hard things in life and it can really knock the wind out of our sails. We are working for the Lord, and something comes along like a death or a tragedy or a diagnosis, or the loss of a job, and it just hurts.

What happens to us? It's kind of like this can.

Squeeze the can. Use both hands and strain a little bit. Put some obvious pressure on it.

It may be uncomfortable, but you can't crush it.

Others in life may experience the same kinds of challenges, but without the Lord, what can happen to them?

Crush the empty, opened can. It should be super-easy to do.

What's the difference in the two cans?

One was filled with something, and one was not. One was filled and one was empty.

If you have God's Spirit inside you, you don't have to be crushed. If you are filled with God's Spirit, you're going to have bad days, but nothing can destroy you. Why? You've got something inside you, keeping you from being crushed.

I think that's a great way for us to introduce our prophet today: Daniel. Most people probably would've been crushed by some of the things that he had to go through, but that wasn't who Daniel was at all. Instead, he was faithful (faithFULL), and because of that faith, he never wavered even when the circumstances around him were anything but stable.

Prophet Profile: Daniel

- Name means "God is my judge." His Babylonian name, "Belteshazzar," meant "protect the king!"
- Was a young man in Jerusalem when the city was overtaken and was carried into Babylon as a prisoner of war.
- Chosen to be a part of King Nebuchadnezzar's "Babylonian education program," where the most outstanding and influential young Israelites were taught the language, literature, and customs of the Chaldeans.
- Had three faithful friends: Shadrach, Meshach, and Abednego.
- Had ability to interpret dreams and strange happenings, like the mysterious hand that appeared and wrote on the wall (Daniel 5). This God-given ability helped him rise to power in Babylon, where King Nebuchadnezzar made him ruler over the entire province and chief among his wise men.
- Had a custom of bowing down and praying to God three times a day.
- Saw the rise and fall of three different Babylonian kings. However, it didn't matter to Daniel which king was seated on the throne of Babylon. His Lord was seated on the throne of his heart.
- Jealous coworkers persecuted him for his strong faith and tried to have him killed by being thrown into a lions' den. God thwarted their plans and rescued him by sending an angel to shut the mouths of the hungry lions.
- Saw strange visions similar to those that we read about John receiving in the Book of Revelation.
- The visions and dreams in Daniel seem to echo an overwhelming message: God's Word and God's kingdom would always stand!

Prophet in Action

When I (Andrew) was in first grade, my parents told me we were moving. They said we would move in with my grandparents while we looked for a place to live, and our moving date would be in three months. Somehow, I misunderstood at first and thought we would be moving in with my grandparents for three months, then going back home. I will never forget the day we registered for my new school, and it dawned on me that we were not going home. After the tears, I realized that this was where I lived now.

Maybe you have experienced a move like that. Maybe a job took your family to a new city, or you moved to another house across town and started a new school. These transitions are not easy. You have to start over—learn your way around, make new friends, figure out new teachers—it can be tough.

Think about it:
What is one of the hardest parts about moving to a new place?

As tough as those times can be, none of us have experienced as dramatic a transition as Daniel did. Israel had been divided into two kingdoms (north and south) for generations. The Assyrians conquered the northern tribes of Israel, completely overwhelming them and scattering Israelite escapees in the area around them. The southern kingdom was conquered by Babylon, but they had a different approach. Instead of scattering them abroad, Babylon would find the most promising people and try to assimilate them—to make them become Babylonians.

This is what happened to Daniel. He was one of the "nobles" of the southern kingdom, which meant he was a young, talented man who was on track to become a leader in Judah. The Babylonians thought that if they could convert that group of young people to the Babylonian culture, it would make Babylon that much stronger. The Babylonians took this group of young people away from the only home they had ever known, trained them to speak a different language, and taught them different subjects in school. That is a serious transition.

In fact, the Babylonians took the vessels out of Judah's temple, which was something nations did to try to prove they have dominance over the god the defeated nation served. They also changed the names of the young people they had taken. Daniel's name became "Belteshazzar." Even with the name change, we still call him by his Hebrew name. There were other name changes. You might not immediately recognize Hananiah, Michael, and Azariah (Hebrew names), but you have probably heard of Shadrach, Meshach, and Abednego (new Babylonian names). The Babylonians hoped that if they could change their names, they would change their identity.

So, how would Daniel respond to this challenge?

He Made a Decision

Daniel 1:8 begins with an important phrase—"Daniel made up his mind" (NASB).

A lot of things in Daniel's life were completely out of his control. There was no way he could keep from being taken out of his home country, and he would have to learn a new language and way of life to be able to survive.

But Daniel looked around and decided there were some things he could control, and one of those was what he ate.

Scripture does not tell us exactly why Daniel and his friends (Shadrach, Meshach, and Abednego) decided not to eat from the king's table, as all the other young nobles were doing. There may have been a couple of different reasons for this. First of all, the Law of Moses required Jews to avoid "unclean" food, and even "clean" food that was prepared improperly. The king's diet may have included those kinds of food. It may also have been that food at the king's table had already been offered to Babylonian gods.

Whatever the reasoning, Daniel saw this as an area where he could take a stand and preserve his identity.

Have you ever felt overwhelmed by the world around you? Maybe you have been sitting in a classroom while students around you made fun of someone for going to church, and you were afraid they might find out about you. Maybe it seems like everyone else at school is hooking up with someone else, and no one seems to think that is wrong. It is easy to feel overwhelmed by circumstances you cannot control, but Daniel decided to find something he could control and refuse to compromise his identity.

Think about it:
What are some specific ways you can make a decision to stand for your Christian identity today?

God was with Daniel and his friends, which is a theme that shows up repeatedly in Daniel. They had a diet of vegetables and water instead of the king's food, and after 10 days, they looked healthier than the others. Not only that, but God gave them wisdom, and Daniel was even given the ability to interpret dreams. When they made the decision to maintain their identity, God was with them.

He Made a Daily Decision

It is easy to make a decision; living out that decision daily is the real challenge. Not only did Daniel decide to be faithful in chapter 1, but he also decided to be faithful every day of his life.

Major changes happen in the next few chapters of Daniel.

In chapters 3 and 4, King Nebuchadnezzar sees God's power and acknowledges Him. Daniel also excelled under Nebuchadnezzar's son Belshazzar, until the Medo-Persian empire overthrew him and Darius the Mede took power. Even under a new ruler and a new occupying nation, Daniel still rose to the top of the ranks, making his coworkers jealous.

In Daniel 6, these jealous coworkers came together to search for an accusation they could make against Daniel in front of the king.

Sharing the Prophets

Just like groups start digging into the background of a candidate who is running for office, they started investigating Daniel. You can imagine why they might be jealous of a foreigner who had risen to such a prominent position in the kingdom. The only problem was that Daniel didn't have any skeletons in his closet; his faithful life meant they couldn't find any dirt on him.

They realized that the only way to find an accusation against him would be to use his faith against him.

Read Daniel 6:6-15 to see how they set their plan into action.

Once they had convinced Darius to sign a law to keep Babylonian citizens from worshipping anyone other than him, they had Daniel trapped. They knew he prayed to God three times a day, which was a common Jewish practice, and they caught him. Darius was grieved by his capture, but once the decree was signed into law, it couldn't be changed.

Here is where we are introduced to the famous lions' den. We have records of Assyrian and Persian kings maintaining lions and hunting them for sport, so these may have been kept for hunting but were eventually used for punishment. Sometimes, children's books show pictures of cute lions sitting in the den with Daniel, but that is not the case. These would have been vicious carnivores; Daniel should have been killed quickly and violently. But that didn't happen.

Check out Daniel 6:16-28 to see what did happen.

Think about it:
What kinds of consequences will we face if we make the daily decision to serve God? How can we prepare ourselves to face them with faith?

Daniel did not die in the lions' den, but his opponents did. In fact, Daniel 6:24 tells us the lions attacked them before they had even made it to the bottom of the pit.

Daniel didn't survive because the lions were not hungry; Daniel survived because the God to whom he faithfully prayed delivered him. Daniel reminds us of the value of daily, faithful decisions.

Looking to Jesus

In the New Testament, there are several phrases that are used to describe Jesus. We often think of terms like Messiah and Son of God, but one Jesus used often was Son of Man. This did not mean "son of a human" (although Jesus was fully divine and fully human). It was a phrase that indicated Jesus' divine identity. Here are a few times we see that phrase show up in the Gospels:

- Matthew 8:20—Jesus said to him, "Foxes have holes and the birds of the air have nests, but the Son of Man has nowhere to lay his head."
- Mark 8:31—He began to teach them that the Son of Man must suffer many things and be rejected by the elders and the chief priests and the scribes, and be killed and after three days rise again.
- Luke 22:48—but Jesus said to him, "Judas, would you betray the Son of Man with a kiss?

That phrase is not only found in the New Testament though, it is actually present in several Old Testament books, and Daniel is one of them. The second half of the book of Daniel contains visions God gave Daniel, and Daniel 7 shows us a vision of a kingdom that will last forever. Once the Ancient of Days (God) is on the throne, the Son of Man comes to receive dominion over the kingdom, in a description that sounds a lot like the way Jesus is pictured in New Testament passages like Philippians 2:9-11.

Listen to how Daniel describes the Son of Man in Daniel 7:13-14: "I kept looking in the night visions, and behold, with the clouds of heaven One like a son of man was coming, and He came up to the Ancient of Days and was presented before Him. And to Him was given dominion, Honor, and a kingdom, so that all the peoples, nations and populations of all languages might serve Him. His dominion is an everlasting dominion which will not pass away; and His kingdom is one which will not be destroyed" (NASB).

Some have stated that Jesus never claimed to be the Son of God. Yet, if we know the way the title "Son of Man" was used in Daniel, we know Jesus is making a clear statement. He is telling everyone that He is the Messiah, and He is the fulfillment of what was promised in Daniel 7.

Prophet Sharing

This week, what if you chose to take the Daniel challenge, making it a point to get on your knees and pray three times a day? A couple of things to keep in mind on this...

1. It isn't about checking off a box.
"I bowed down on my knees and prayed three times today! Check! Done! Next!"

Prayer is not meant to be something you "just do." It is meant to be a time of pouring out your heart to God. So do that!

2. If you "fail" in this challenge, you really haven't failed.
"Oh no! I only got on my knees and prayed once today! I AM A COMPLETE SPIRITUAL FAILURE!"

Hey, if you spent time pouring out your heart to God even once today, you haven't failed at all. Please don't base your spiritual success/failure solely upon this exercise.

I do, however, hope you'll give this a shot, bearing in mind the great discipline of Daniel, who made this so much more than a daily routine.

Hosea: The PROPHET Who Married a Prostitute

Mystery Object: WEDDING RING

A wedding ring serves as a reminder of a great covenant. Perhaps it would've reminded Hosea of Gomer's unfaithfulness and of Israel's failure to honor their covenant with God. Yet it also would remind him of God's faithfulness, forgiveness, mercy, and love and how He would take Israel back time and time again.

Ice Breakers

Option 1: Mr./Mrs. Right

Take a minute to hand out some paper and pens, and have the students in your class give some thought to what qualities would be good to look for in a future spouse.

Give them a minute to gather some thoughts, then read aloud some of their responses. Some of these answers will probably be entertaining, no matter what the ages of your students are!

Say something like:

You know, what's interesting is that although there were some similarities and differences in these responses, nobody wrote down that they were looking for a spouse that they couldn't trust. Nobody wrote down that they'd really love to have a husband/wife that cheated on them. Nobody said that they were looking for someone who would cause them (and their children) to feel the pain and betrayal of adultery.

Nobody wants that in their love story. In today's study, you're going to meet a prophet you may not have ever studied before named Hosea. What's crazy about him is that he was told to marry a prostitute, a woman who would be unfaithful to him.

Option 2: Weird Baby Names

Say something like:

The prophet we are going to study had a couple of kids with interesting names, so I thought we'd begin class today by sharing with you some of the weirdest baby names I could find[1].

1. **Anna...**: Yep, Anna with an ellipsis at the end! What word, sentence, and section did the parents omit from her name?!? I have to know this!
2. **Britney Shakira Beyonce**: This name belongs to one person. The parents were huge fans of these three singers and couldn't decide whom to name their daughter after. So, they named her Britney Shakira Beyoncé. And, what's even funnier is that they call her full name every single time.
3. **Beberly**: Not Beverly. Beberly.
4. **Abcde**
5. **Merica**: (And now some of you are thinking of naming your child this.)
6. **Facebook**: In Egypt, Jamal Ibrahim named his baby girl Facebook to acknowledge the role the social media played in spurring the revolution in his country. He wanted to pay gratitude to Facebook for helping the people get rid of the President Hosni Mubarak.
7. **Olive Garden**: The father liked the name Garden for their baby girl, but the wife was adamant on Olive. The couple compromised and named her Olive Garden Smith.

[1]Source: https://www.momjunction.com/articles/worst-baby-names-in-the-world_00400377/#gref

8. **Like**: A young couple was so much obsessed with Facebook that they decided to name their son Like, after the Like feature of Facebook.
9. **Hashtag**

Say something like:

Today's prophet could've had a couple of his kids' names on this list: They were named "Not my people" and "No mercy!" Go ahead and turn to the book of Hosea.

Prophet Profile: Hosea

- Name means "salvation."
- Prophet in Northern Kingdom of Israel who prophesied during the reign of Jeroboam II, an arrogant king who adopted the name of the Northern Kingdom's first king, the one who led them into sin.
- Began prophesying after Amos and continued into the reign of Hezekiah.
- Told to take "a wife of whoredom and have children of whoredom," to illustrate how Israel had committed whoredom by forsaking the Lord (1:2).
- Wife named Gomer. Her name means "complete" and may symbolize the "complete wickedness" of Israel.
- Had a son named Jezreel (name means "God scatters"), a daughter named Lo-ruhama ("No mercy"), and another son named "Lo-ammi" ("Not my people"). Read 2:16-23 to see what God says about the names of Hosea's children here.
- Even though Hosea's wife was unfaithful to him, he bought her back. This symbolized God's desire to redeem Israel, even though they continually committed spiritual adultery against him, turning aside to idols.

Sharing the Prophets

Prophet in Action

It was not a pleasant place. You have to wonder what was going through his mind as he walked through it.

Yes, these places were part of the culture at the time, but a slave auction would still have been unbearable. Having conversations with sellers without making eye contact with the slaves in question, seeing the mistreatment that some had suffered, trying not to think of the stories in their lives that had led them to this point—it would have been more than unpleasant; it would have been unbearable. It would not have been a place we normally expect to find love, but it is there, at a slave auction.

We know what we normally expect from a love story; we have seen plenty of them. When we watch most movies, we know that two people will fall in love and no matter what, all their problems will be solved by the end of the movie. We check out Instagram feeds of our favorite celebrities who update us on their romantic status by posting pictures that have been carefully chosen and retouched through just the right filter. Even something that used to be done in private, a marriage proposal, is recorded on video and posted online minutes after it happens.

We know the usual setting and environment for love, but Hosea 3 creates a different context for love: a slave auction.

Hosea was a prophet who lived in the eighth century. By this time, Israel had been divided into northern and southern kingdoms, and Hosea prophesied during the final days of the northern kingdom of Israel. Israel had been unfaithful to God for many years, and they were about to receive their punishment, being conquered by Assyria. In the middle of this turbulent time, God asks Hosea to do something drastic to illustrate Israel's unfaithfulness. To understand this setting, we will need to start at the beginning of the book of Hosea.

Read Hosea 1:1-2 to understand Hosea's mission from God.

Understanding Unfaithfulness

God gives Hosea a tough command here; he tells Hosea to marry a prostitute. In fact, that term is used multiple times in verse 2, as if to emphasize how difficult this would be. He marries a woman named Gomer, and in chapter 2, it becomes clear that she has left Hosea and is unfaithful to him.

Some question whether Gomer was a prostitute when Hosea married her or if that took place later. Either way, God made it clear from the beginning what would happen, and He was at work to illustrate something powerful through Hosea's life.

After Hosea marries Gomer, she has three children. The birth of a child is usually a joyous time, but Hosea 1 tells a different story. In fact, it isn't clear that Hosea is the father of all three. Verse 3 clearly states that the first son is Hosea's ("bore him a son"), but that phrase doesn't show up when the other two are described. It may be that Gomer's unfaithfulness had already started.

No matter what, Hosea certainly loved and raised all three of the children, even when Gomer left. When you read the names of this children, you will be reminded of two things: Baby names have changed a lot since the eighth century, and the meanings of these names tell us some important things. At the time this is being written, the most popular baby boy name is Jackson, and the most popular baby girl name is Sophia. Compare that to these names from the first chapter of Hosea: Jezreel, Lo-ruhamah, and Lo-ammi. Sounds a little different, doesn't it?

When parents choose the name of a child today, they are usually thinking about how names sound or maybe preserving the name of a family member. In the Bible, parents would often think about the meaning behind a name. The meanings behind these names reveal a message from God. Jezreel means "God scatters." The people of Israel had been unfaithful to God, and they would be "scattered" when the Assyrians conquered them. The second child was Lo-ruhamah, a name which means "no mercy," and the third was Lo-ammi, a name which means "not my people." God is sending a clear signal that since Israel was unfaithful, they would no longer be God's people.

To complete the picture of unfaithfulness, Gomer leaves in Hosea 2:5. It would be hard to imagine a worse situation for Hosea.

Think about it:
What are some ways sin can damage our lives and leave us in situations that seem hopeless?

Understanding Our Unfaithfulness

It is easy to name all the ways Israel was being unfaithful to God. In fact, Hosea 4 tells us they were doing all kinds of things: disregarding God's commands, believing false prophets, and worshiping idols. It is a little bit harder for us to name ways we are unfaithful, but we know they exist, right?

Think about it:
Can you think of some examples of unfaithfulness that we don't talk about much? Why do we avoid those subjects?

Hosea 4:1 says there was no faithfulness in the land of Israel. God had communicated what He wanted them to do, but they had chosen not to do it.

Do we ever do that? Have you ever avoided someone at school or made fun of another student just so people wouldn't make fun of you? If we know that God wants us to show His love to others, yet we don't do it, aren't we doing what Israel did?

Hosea 4:6 tells us that people rejected the knowledge of God. If we know what God's Word teaches about sexuality, we will realize that our culture teaches something different. Instead of God's standards that reserve sex for marriage between a man and woman, it would be easier just to say whatever culture tells us is right. If we do that, aren't we also rejecting the knowledge of God?

The Israelites were worshipping idols, which sounds strange to us. We might even feel good about ourselves, grateful that we don't do something as foolish as bowing down before an idol. But the essence of idolatry is that human beings were putting the love and worship of something else in place of their faithfulness to God.

If I allow something in my life to dominate my time, money, and energy in place of my faithfulness to God, aren't I doing the same thing?

Understanding God's Redeeming Love

As God planned, Hosea responds to Gomer's unfaithfulness with redeeming love. In fact, the word redeem means "to buy back," and that is exactly what Hosea does. A slave auction doesn't seem like the place to find love, but Hosea 3 shows how it happens. After leaving him, Gomer has found herself in slavery, and Hosea 3:2 tells us that Hosea bought her back for 15 shekels and some barley. She was the wife who had left him, become a slave, and now he was buying her back.

It's hard to imagine a more powerful picture of love.

You might have heard about Helen Keller, a woman who was born in 1880 who lost both her sight and her hearing from a sickness she contracted at 19 months old. She would often tell the story of how she learned to communicate. Her teacher, Anne Sullivan, would hand her a doll, then trace the word D-O-L-L on her hand. That taught her not only how to spell, but what different words meant. After she had learned hundreds of words, Anne Sullivan traced the word L-O-V-E. Anne traced back the sentence, "What is love?" This wasn't something she could touch and feel; it was a concept she would have to learn a different way.

Hosea is more than just the story of a prophet from ancient Israel. It is a picture of love. What is love?

The way Hosea treated Gomer—that is love.

Sharing the Prophets

Looking to Jesus

In John 8, when Jesus was talking to a crowd of Jews who were proud of their heritage as descendants of Abraham, He points out their unfaithfulness. In John 8:34, Jesus said, "Truly, truly I say to you, everyone who practices sin is a slave to sin." When we sin, it is like we are enslaved to it—we are allowing that sin to control our actions.

Think about it:
Can you think of some sins that cause people to say and do things they would never normally say or do?

Human beings were created by God, and when sin entered the world in Genesis 3, something happened that is important to understand. We were separated from God by sin, and we became slaves to sin. That is why Romans 3:24 describes God's grace this way: "being justified as a gift by His grace through the redemption which is in Christ Jesus" (NASB).

There's that word—*redemption*.

Through Jesus' sacrifice, sinful people are "bought back." God made us, we left Him, and He bought us back.

That is redeeming love.

Prophet Sharing

Hosea sheds light into an important area that we don't usually talk about in a class with teenagers: marriage. Do you ever pray for your future spouse? Now would be a great time to start. Pray that you will find a partner who will be faithful to you and to the Lord, and pray that you will be the same kind of partner for your spouse.

Jonah: The Fish Food PROPHET

Mystery Object: FISH

You could...

- Bring a live fish in a fish bowl.
- Bring a fake fish.
- Use "Let's Go Fishin'!" if you are using Ice Breaker Option #1.

Ice Breakers

Option 1: Let's Go Fishin'!
This one is pretty old-fashioned I suppose, but it's quick, easy, and straight to the point.

All you need to do is locate the classic children's game, "Let's Go Fishin'!" Do you remember that game, with the little fishing poles and the fish that spin and around and open and shut their mouths? Pick some volunteers who will face off, and see who can collect the most fish before they are all gone. Winner wins whatever you decide.

After the game, say something like:
I thought we'd begin by doing a little fishing this morning since today we are going to be studying a prophet by the name of Jonah.

Option 2: I Don't Care What Simon Says
This one is going to mess with people's minds, but essentially this is "Simon Says" in reverse! Basically, whenever someone says "Simon Says" you do the complete opposite of what the person says.

Example: "Simon says raise your hand."
Correct response: Do not raise your hand.
Incorrect response: Raise your hand.
Example: "Raise your hand."
Correct response: Raise your hand.
Incorrect response: Don't raise your hand.

Again, basically, you ignore whatever Simon Says.

After you've played this for a couple of minutes, say something like:

"This game is sort of a challenge, isn't it? We are so used to doing whatever Simon says that it feels weird to do the exact opposite. Today we're going to talk about a prophet who basically did the exact opposite of what God said he needed to do. His name is Jonah."

Prophet Profile: Jonah

- Name means "dove."
- Told to preach to Nineveh, an incredibly wicked city. Jonah has other plans and is swallowed by a great fish for disobeying God. The fish becomes his home for three days.
- Chapter 2 features a beautiful prayer that Jonah speaks from inside the belly of the fish.
- Jonah displays a variety of emotions, from anger to joy, then from joy to disgust. Jonah reminds us how fickle, selfish, and even dramatic we can be at times in the grand scheme of things.
- Jesus makes a cool comparison between him and Jonah, saying just as Jonah spent three days in the belly of a fish, he would spend three days in the belly of the earth (a tomb) before he would rise from the grave.

Sharing the Prophets

Prophet in Action

Not too long ago, Richard Schimpf, a 51-year-old dive tour operator, was in the water off the coast of South Africa photographing a school of sardines. As he got closer to the sardines, he was suddenly plunged into darkness. Richard soon realized that a whale had been after the swimming mass of sardines and had scooped him up as well. Though the Bryde's whale (a species of whale that not widely known) are known for taking in a mouthful of water, then straining out the fish they would like to eat. The whale spat Schimpf out after only a couple of seconds, which is what these whales do any time they scoop up an inedible animal with their meal. Richard was physically fine, and he went on the Today Show to recount his incredible story.

It isn't surprising that reporters referenced the prophet Jonah when they talked about this event; it was almost inevitable. When we think about Jonah, we often picture him alongside a big fish, as if that is the entire story of Jonah. But Jonah is more than a story about a fish, it is a story about humanity. It is a story about us, and the way we often resist God's commands or resent God's grace. As we read Jonah, let's not think so much about the fish that we lose sight of God.

We are introduced to Jonah in 2 Kings 14:25. He was the son of a man named Amittai, who came from an area just a few miles north of Nazareth, where Jesus would live. God calls in Jonah to do something that would have been uncomfortable for a prophet from Nazareth—preach to Nineveh.

That might sound like a natural mission; isn't telling God's message to others part of the prophet's job description? But Nineveh was not like any of the other cities in Jonah's time. Jonah 1:2 tells us that Nineveh was filled with wickedness, and it was a major Assyrian city. Assyria was an enemy of the northern kingdom of Israel, and preaching to them would be like preaching behind enemy lines. Yet that is exactly what God tells him to do.

Read Jonah 1:1-17 to see what happens.

Think about it:
What are some examples of commands in Scripture that seem to go against our natural tendencies?

What Happens When We Resist God's Plan?

Jonah's initial reaction was resistance. His first step was not in Nineveh's direction, but the opposite one. Nineveh was located to the east, but Jonah went straight to Joppa, directly to the west. In fact, Jonah 1:3 tells us that Jonah found a ship and went down into it "to go with them…from the presence of the LORD."

His goal was clear: He was trying to escape God's presence, but he was going to find out that was impossible. In fact, Psalm 139:7 shows us how hopeless that is, asking the question, "Where can I go from Your Spirit? Or where can I flee from Your presence?" (NASB)

Picture a two-year old boy playing hide and seek, thinking he can hide from everyone just by covering his eyes. We would laugh, knowing that won't work. Guess what didn't work for Jonah. Climbing into a boat.

God knew where Jonah was, and He got Jonah's attention. While Jonah was asleep in the boat, God sent a storm so violent that the ship was almost broken. Verse 5 tells us that even these experienced sailors were so scared that they began throwing cargo off the ship and praying to the gods they served. The captain woke Jonah and asked him to pray to his God. When that didn't work, they tried to find out who was responsible for the storm by casting lots. Think about that. The storm was so bad that a seasoned crew was convinced it is divine punishment for someone.

Jonah finally admitted to them that he was running away from God's presence, and he told the crew to throw him overboard. They picked him up and threw him into the sea. In fact, verses 4 and 15 use the same Hebrew term; God "hurled" a great wind on the sea and the sailors "hurled" Jonah into the water. In chapter 2, Jonah describes being in the heart of the sea, engulfed by water and his head wrapped up by seaweed. It seems like Jonah was drowning and thought he was close to death before what happened next.

This is the part of the story most people know; Jonah was swallowed by a fish. We don't know exactly what type of fish it was, but we know it was prepared by God for this purpose. If you read chapter 2, you can listen to Jonah's prayer from the stomach of the fish. Can you imagine the desperation Jonah would have felt? He tells God that he will be faithful.

Think about it:
Has there been a time in your life when prayed out of desperation? How did that feel?

Jonah had initially resisted God's plan, but God did get his attention. His story isn't over, though.

Think about it:
Can you think of anything God calls Christians to do that we might resist?

What Happens When We Reject God's Plan?

In Jonah 3:1, God comes to Jonah a second time with the same command. This time, Jonah does what God says. He goes to Nineveh with a simple message: "Yet forty days and Nineveh shall be overthrown" (3:4). That sentence may be only eight words long in English, but it is even shorter in its original language. The Old Testament was written in Hebrew, and only four words sum up the message God had for Nineveh.

Judgment was coming to Nineveh, and Nineveh took this message seriously. The people in Nineveh began fasting, and they put on sack cloth, which was a symbol of mourning for them. The king of Nineveh issued a proclamation that even the animals would not eat or drink while they prayed to God that they would not die.

Sharing the Prophets

The powerful effect of this simple message is impressive. There are times when God's message might seem basic or routine to us, yet God's simple message still has power.

Think about it:
What are some commands of God that are simple yet powerful?

So far, everything is going well. Jonah has obeyed God, he has preached God's message, and people are responding. That should make someone feel good right?

Read Jonah 4:1-11 to find out how Jonah reacted.

Isn't that surprising? Jonah is a prophet, and prophets are supposed to rejoice when people obey God, aren't they? Jonah does the opposite. His response to God is like a child pouting when he doesn't get what he wants; he tells God essentially, "I knew this would happen." He is so upset that Nineveh could be forgiven by God that he no longer wanted to live.

Think about that:
How upset would you have to be to say that? How angry would you have to be at a nation to wish they would be destroyed rather than saved?

God responds with an object lesson. Just like he raised up a fish, God caused a plant to grow so large that it would provide shade over Jonah's head. It was extremely hot, and Jonah was thankful for the shade. But the next day, God caused a worm to eat the plant, which made Jonah furious. God then asked Jonah a simple question: "Do you have a right to be angry?" After all, God made the plant. Jonah had nothing to do with it. Why was he angry when it was gone?

The point was obvious. God created every nation in the world, including Nineveh. God alone had the right to forgive them. Who was Jonah to say God couldn't do that? Even after everything he had experienced, Jonah was still rejecting God's plan.

The point for us might be less obvious, but it's just as important. Has there ever been someone in your class at church who has done or said something terrible to you, and then she asked for forgiveness? Sometimes, even though we know we should forgive, we still harbor thoughts that she might not deserve forgiveness. Maybe someone comes back to the church after being away for years, and you are still tempted to hold his past actions against him.

God's reminder to Jonah is His reminder to us: God alone can forgive, and when He does, we must accept it. Jonah needed to accept it, and so do we.

Looking to Jesus

During Jesus' ministry, He often used parables to help people to discuss spiritual principles. Parables were stories that challenged assumptions and provoked insights. One of the most well-known parables is the Prodigal Son.

Before we think about this parable, we need to remember who is listening. In Luke 15:1-2, we read that all the sinners and tax collectors (who were looked down on by most people in the first century) were coming to Jesus, which caused the Pharisees to start grumbling about the kind of people hanging around Jesus. This prompted Jesus to start telling parables about people searching for lost things, a lost sheep and a lost coin.

His third parable is about a young man who asks for his inheritance early, essentially sending the message that he doesn't want to wait for his father to die. ("Hi, Dad. Let's pretend that life is already like it will be when you're dead. I don't feel like waiting.") The son lives it up and spends all his money, then realizes he has nowhere to go. He takes a job feeding pigs and comes to his senses, realizing that even the day laborers at his father's house were doing better than he was.

Sharing the Prophets

When he returns home, his father runs to meet him, giving him a robe, a ring, and sandals, which represented the son's return as a full-fledged member of the family. The father throws a party for his lost son, which makes the older brother angry. Listen to what the older brother says to the father in Luke 15:29-30, "Look, these many years I have served you, and I never disobeyed your command, yet you never gave me a young goat, that I might celebrate with my friends. But when this son of yours came, who has devoured your property with prostitutes, you killed the fattened calf for him!"

The older brother was angry because his father forgave someone else. Does that sound familiar? That is exactly what Jonah was doing; he was pouting because God forgave people Jonah thought did not deserve it. In fact, this is the same feeling the Pharisees had when they saw Jesus reaching out to sinners and tax collectors. They didn't think they deserved to be treated that way by a religious leader. After all, Pharisees didn't reach out to them that way. As they heard Jesus describe the older brother, they were hearing Jesus describe their attitude.

What each of the parables in Luke 15 reminds us of is that when someone (or something) lost is found, there is rejoicing. The implication is that when someone, anyone, who is lost comes back to God, He rejoices like the father who runs to meet his son.

Just like the book of Jonah, the parable of the Prodigal Son is open-ended. Jonah 4 does not tell us how Jonah reacts to God's object lesson. We are left to imagine Jonah's response. The parable of the Prodigal Son does not tell us how the older brother responds to his father. We are left to imagine his response. This is fitting because our own stories are open-ended. The way we respond to God's forgiveness is up to us.

What will we do when someone who has hurt us is forgiven by God? How will we respond when a person who has caused pain in the lives of family members comes back to the Lord?

Sharing the Prophets

The choice is ours.

Prophet Sharing

Perhaps there have been times when we have wanted to run in the opposite direction instead of doing what God has told us to do. Is there something you have been avoiding that you need to face? What can you do to run toward that responsibility today instead of away from it?

Sharing the Prophets

Micah: The Justice-Seeking PROPHET

Mystery Objects: **A BLINDFOLD, A HEART WITH THE WORD *MERCY* WRITTEN ON IT,** AND **A PAIR OF SHOES**

Explanation: The blindfold represents justice (justice is blind), the heart represents "loving mercy," and the shoes represent "walking humbly" with God (Micah 6:8 "...do justice, love mercy, walk humbly with your God," NIV).

Ice Breakers

Option 1: The House Always Wins
For this ice breaker, you'll need a coin, so have one ready.

Ask your class if they think that you can successfully win a coin toss 100% of the time. See if any of them will challenge you.

For this to work right, you'll need to say this key phrase, and say it quickly, so that the person you're playing against doesn't have time to process it.

Just before you flip the coin, quickly say, *"Ok. Heads I win. Tails you lose. Ready?"*

Flip the coin.

Say "It's heads. I win! Next!" (Or "It's tails. You lose!")

You have probably figured this out, but whatever it lands on, you win! At this point, you can either dismiss this person and get a new challenger or rematch the same person. Do this trick over and over until they catch on.   Some will probably catch on faster than others. Even if you get caught, don't let on like you were cheating ("What are you talking about? I called it fair and square. You heard me.")

After the trick has been discovered, say something like:
How many of you like to play games with people who cheat? None of us, right? We expect people to play by the rules. However sometimes in life we run across people who don't think the rules apply to them: people who are corrupt, judges who take bribes, people in authority who abuse the system, teachers who practice favoritism, police officers who break the law they've promised to uphold, and politicians who cross lines to get what they want.

Unfortunately, people like that exist, and they always have. In today's story, we are going to read about a prophet named Micah who was not afraid to speak out against corrupt leaders who oppressed, mistreated, and cheated other people.

Option 2: Little Known Facts

Distribute some pens and slips of paper to your students, and say something like:
"We are going to play a quick game called 'Little Known Facts.' Here's how it works. I want you to write down on this little slip of paper one little known fact about yourself. Something that most people do not know about you. Don't write your name on it and don't show it to anybody. But when you finish, pass it to me, and we are going to see if we can correctly solve your secret identity."

(For example, the paper might say, "I have eaten a worm." The class has to decide who they think is the person who has eaten a worm.)

After the class votes on who-they-think-did-what, say something like:

"Most of us have probably at least heard of the name "Micah" in God's Word, at the very least, because his name is attached to a book of the Bible. But what do you really know about him or about the messages that God told him to proclaim? It's my hope today to be able to better introduce him to you, and though there are "little known facts" about him, he is an impressive, if under-the-radar, prophet."

Prophet Profile: Micah

- Micah's name, a shortened form of Micaiah, means, "Who is like the Lord?"
- From Moresheth-Gath, which is mentioned only here in the Bible.
- Prophet from the southern kingdom who saw everything that happened to the northern kingdom, including its destruction.
- There's actually another Micah mentioned in God's Word in the book of Judges, and if you were to read about him, you'd learn that they are definitely not the same Micah!
- We don't know anything about his personal call to prophecy, but he is characterized by his courage (he was ready and willing to suffer), and he was righteously angered by injustice.

Prophet in Action

All prophets are called to speak out against injustice, and Micah spoke out against some specific things that were happening…

There were "land-grabbers" who would stay awake at night trying to figure out a scheme to trick other people out of their land (Micah 2:1-5). Remember, in the ancient world, land was vital to survival.

There were also rulers who hated good and loved evil instead of providing justice (Micah 3:1-3). These evil practices were not limited to non-religious people.

There were some false prophets who prophesied for money. These prophets would give you good news if you paid them and declare war on you if they didn't like you (Micah 3:5-8).

Some priests did something similar, such as teaching for hire instead of relying on God (Micah 3:11).

In the middle of all of this, Micah knew that the truth needed to be heard.

Think about it:
If Micah looked around the place where you live, what practices would he identify as evil?

Picture yourself walking into a courtroom. You can see the seat at the front for the judge, the wooden rails surrounding the jury box, as well as all the chairs for the spectators. Even if you have not spent time in a courtroom, chances are that you have seen enough television shows or movies to know what happens. A lawyer will "make the case," laying out the evidence for someone's conviction. In Micah 6, God makes His case before Israel, recounting everything He had done for them. As you read Micah 6:1-5, look for the various ways God is making His case.

God's Case Against Israel

God brought up His people from Israel. He delivered them from slavery in Egypt, and the Israelites responded by longing for Egypt. They dreamed about the plentiful food in Egypt, conveniently forgetting about the backbreaking slave labor they suffered.

God gave them leaders like Moses and Aaron, as well as kings, judges, and prophets. The Israelites would follow these leaders for a time, but they would continually turn their backs on God, ignoring His leaders.

Sharing the Prophets

God had prevented Balak, the king of Moab, from cursing Israel. But Israel answered by intermarrying and falling into idol worship.

Each step of the way, God was the One who gave them a way forward, but Israel kept moving backward.

Now, let's bring this case into our world today. What would be God's case against us?

God delivered the Israelites from slavery in Egypt, and God has delivered us from slavery to sin (Romans 6:17). Do we ever complain about God's commands? Do we ever think longingly about what it would be like not to have those rules, conveniently forgetting about the consequences of sin?

God has also given us leaders to guide us, from the inspired authors of Scripture to the elders of our congregations. What good does that guidance do if we turn our backs on it? In fact, God often protects us in ways we might not know or realize, yet we often willfully sin and enter to harmful areas that God has kept us from encountering.

Think about it:
We aren't as different from the Israelites as we might think we are. What are some other similarities between the Israelites and us?

Israel's Solution
Read verses 6 and 7.

We can imagine the Israelites responding with possible ways to make things right.

Would more burnt offerings help? In 1 Kings 3:4, King Solomon sacrificed 1,000 burnt offerings. In 1 Kings 8:5, when the ark of the covenant was taken into the temple, Solomon sacrificed so many sheep and oxen that they could not be counted. Yet God makes it clear that not even a Solomon-sized sacrifice could get the job done.

Would thousands of rams or rivers of oil solve everything? Rams were used for guilt offerings in the Old Testament, to atone for sins. But there were not enough rams in all of Israel to atone for what they had done.

What about offering a firstborn? Though it is true that God tested Abraham by asking him to sacrifice his son Isaac, God did not let Abraham go through with it. Child sacrifice was a practice of pagan worship, and it was not something God asked His people to do.

Micah is not downplaying the importance of sacrifice, but he is reminding them that they have to live faithfully as well, which they were not doing.

Let's put ourselves in Israel's place: What could we offer to earn God's forgiveness?

Should we just try to attend more worship services or more Bible classes?

What if we sing louder or give more?

All these things are good, and we should be doing them, but these outward acts do not do enough if they are not joined by a moral life.

Have you ever known someone who knew how to do and say all the right things in Bible class but didn't live that way during the week? Our life needs to match our actions, and even then, we could never do enough to earn the forgiveness we need.

God's Solution
In verse 8, we see a famous verse from Micah that describes how God's people should live. This is God's design for walking with Him:

1. Do justice.
After listing all the ways that would not work, God specifies what He asks of His people. He wanted them to do justice. Later in the chapter, God will describe the way rich people were swindling other

people out of their money through "dishonest scales," tricking people into paying more than they should for goods they needed.

This is a consistent theme in the minor prophets; God cares about how people treat one another, especially those who are poor. Another Old Testament prophet named Amos would say, "Let justice roll down like waters, and righteousness like an ever-flowing stream," (Amos 5:24).

Have you ever wondered why we know, deep down, it is important to take care of people in need? Even people who don't believe in God know that we should help others. We were made in the image of God, and justice has always mattered to God.

2. Love mercy.
Maybe you have played the game "Mercy" before, where two people try to squeeze each other's hands as hard as possible, to see who will be the first to say the word mercy. We sometimes limit the idea of mercy to helping people when they are in serious trouble, but this word means something bigger than that. *Mercy* can also be translated "lovingkindness," the kind of love God has shown us.

3. Walk humbly.
The term Micah uses here could be translated "modestly" or "cautiously." With each step we take in life, we need to be watching ourselves to make sure our pride doesn't get out of control. Micah was talking to people in power who were abusing their power and profiting off others. If they humbled themselves enough to respond to Micah's prophecy, then they could put their lives back on the right track.

Think about it:
Why is it so easy to let our pride get the best of us? What should we do to stay humble?

Looking to Jesus

Micah 6:8 gives us a template for how to live, so it shouldn't surprise us to see that Jesus lived it out in the Gospels. Justice clearly mattered to Jesus.

In Matthew 21, Jesus saw the crowd of people in the temple who were changing money (for those who traveled from out of town and needed money for the temple offerings) and selling doves for sacrifices. They were so focused on doing business, and likely overcharging others, that they lost sight of the purpose of the temple. Jesus overturned the tables and cleared them from the temple.

In His ministry, Jesus was constantly reaching out to people on the fringes of society who the religious leaders avoided. Jesus wanted justice to be offered to everyone.

Jesus is the definition of mercy. When we think of a description of God's love in the New Testament, John 3:16 is a verse that often comes to mind. But there is another John 3:16 passage that illustrates His "lovingkindness": 1 John 3:16.

Take a few minutes to read 1 John 3:16-18. Just as Jesus laid down His life for us, we are called to do the same thing. He personifies mercy, and He calls us to show mercy to others.

When it comes to humility, Jesus shows us how to live it out. When Paul describes Jesus' mission in Philippians 2, he states that Jesus humbled Himself by being obedient to death on a cross. Crucifixion was created by the Romans to show their power over their subjects, and criminals were usually the ones taken to a cross against their will. Yet that wasn't true for Jesus. As Jesus told Pilate in John 19:11, Pilate would have no power over Jesus unless it had been given to him from above. Jesus had the power to say no to the cross, yet He was willing to humble Himself to the point of crucifixion to fulfill God's plan.

If Jesus was willing to do that for us, what should we be willing to do for others?

Prophet Sharing

Think for a moment about what it means to love justice. Is there someone you know of who is being denied justice? Pray for them.

Think about what it means to love mercy (or kindness). Do you know someone who could use a little kindness right now? How can you show them kindness?

Think about what it means to walk humbly with God. What is something you can do for the glory of God today that would bring Him honor—not something others will see, but something only God will see?

Sharing the Prophets

Habakkuk: The PROPHET with Messy Questions

Mystery Item/Ice Breaker: MESSY QUESTIONS

Take a minute to hand out paper and pens and have the students in your class answer this question. "If you could ask God one question, what would it be?"

Let the students know...
1. They can put their name on the paper if they'd like, but isn't necessary.
2. You'd like to read these responses aloud, but you will not say who wrote what.

Take all the students' questions, put them inside a box, shuffle them, and read them out loud. (You may get some funny questions in there, too! Nothing wrong with those questions either!)

When you have read through their responses (or at least some of them), put them all back inside the box and dump them onto the floor so that it makes a pretty good mess (you may need to add your own questions to the mix to get the full messy effect).

The mystery item this week is "messy questions." Here's why...

1. Habakkuk was a prophet who had questions for God that are similar to many questions we might like to ask God today: "Why do bad things seem to happen to good people?" "Where is justice?" "Why do the bad guys seem to be winning?"

2. This can also represent that questions can cause a mess if we don't handle them the right way (Habakkuk did, by the way).

Say something like:
Life is filled with tough questions, isn't it? We may never know the answer to many of them. But here's what's awesome: We serve a God who is not afraid of our questions. In fact, He goes so far as to say to us, "Seek and you shall find." It isn't wrong to ask God tough questions, but it's important for us to "seek Him" in our answers.

Today we're going to study a prophet named Habakkuk who wrestled with some difficult questions when it came to understanding God's plans.

Prophet Profile: Habakkuk

- Name means "embrace."
- Probably lived around the same time as Jeremiah and had a front row seat to the suffering of Israel.
- There is practically nothing known about Habakkuk's backstory. A couple of fun legends about him are (1) that he could be the sneezing son of the Shunnamite woman that Elisha raised from the dead, or (2) he could be the watchman that Isaiah appointed in Isaiah 21:6 (see language used in Habakkuk 2:1).

Prophet in Action

There are certain things human beings just know. From an early age, children will often smile back at people who smile at them. They don't have to be told to do that; they just know. Both of my (Andrew's) sons could identify the sound of a candy bar unwrapping from an early age. They might never have seen that particular kind of candy bar before, but when they heard their father unwrap it, they would run toward the sound as fast as their

Sharing the Prophets

little legs would carry them. No one had to teach them that candy bars tasted good. They just knew.

Another thing we recognize instinctively is when something in life isn't fair.

Your friend talks all the time during class, but as soon as you talk back, you are the one who gets in trouble. It isn't fair.

Players on the other basketball team are fouling your school's players constantly, but they never get called for it. As soon as one of your players brushes up against someone else, the whistle blows and a foul is called. It isn't fair.

You work hard on a paper, but you forgot the teacher told you to format it a certain way, and you lose points. Meanwhile, the girl who sits next to you did the same thing, and the teacher missed it, giving her full credit. It isn't fair.

No one has to tell us that. We just know.

As frustrating as those challenges can be, our questions of fairness become even more serious as we mature. We see people who are unkind, only concerned for themselves, and nothing bad ever seems to happen to them. Yet we are close to wonderful, loving Christians who are having to deal with serious challenges. That doesn't seem fair.

Think about it:
What are some things you see in life that just aren't fair?

We are not the first people to ask that question. One of the biblical prophets named Habakkuk asked the same question, because he was watching God's people suffer. Although we don't know many details about Habakkuk's life, we know that he likely lived around the time of another prophet we have already talked about, Jeremiah. (Remember, he was called the "weeping prophet.") This means he had a front row seat to the captivity of God's people by the Babylonians. His book is different than other books of prophecy, because he doesn't give a message to God's people. Instead, his book records a conversation between Habakkuk and God.

The Babylonians were powerful, and when they took Judah captive, they also took captive the articles in the temple, as if to say that their gods were more powerful than the God of Judah. Habakkuk would certainly have known that the nation of Judah had struggled with faithfulness, but the Babylonians didn't even believe in God. Why would God allow the Babylonians to flourish and His own people to suffer?

So, how does Habakkuk get to the point that he would trust in God in the middle of all these questions? How does he maintain his faith even when he doesn't completely understand why God is allowing certain things to happen? His prayer in chapter three gives us some guidelines. These principles can help us when we struggle with tough questions. Let's remember two things:

1. Remember what God has done.
Take a few minutes to read part of Habakkuk's prayer in Habakkuk 3:1-6.

Since this is a passage from a different culture than ours, you will probably notice some words you don't read often and names of places we don't talk about daily. For example, "Selah" is a musical term that often shows up in the psalms, and the term "Shigionoth" indicates that this is a prayer set to music, much like the psalms. Read these verses, and ask yourself what Habakkuk is saying about God.

Habakkuk begins by remembering God's power in creation. He says that it causes him to "fear." This is not the kind of fear that causes someone to scream after seeing a spider. The type of fear he is citing is a reverence, or holy awe, in the presence of God's power. We might remember the way Isaiah responded in Isaiah 6, when he was in the throne room. Being reminded of God's power should cause us to fear him. Being reminded of God's power in creation should also cause to recognize our own limitation, like Habakkuk did.

Think about it:
What are some aspects of the world around us that display God's power?

When was the last time we reflected on what our world teaches us about God's power? Today, it is easy for us to be separated from nature. We live in air-conditioned buildings, we can go to a grocery store instead of growing our own food, and we have a dry place when it rains. In Habakkuk's time, there were fewer layers between human beings and the world around them. Some of our spiritual mountaintop experiences occur where we feel close to nature, and that probably is not a coincidence. The natural world can show us God's power.

As Habakkuk describes God's power, he also describes God revealing Himself in the wilderness against the nations. Remember, Habakkuk had seen the Babylonians defeat Judah. It was important for him to remember the power God has over all nations. When God led the Israelites into Canaan, they defeated all kinds of enemies, not because they were the strongest or most powerful nation, but because God was powerful, and He was on their side.

Think about it:
What are some things God has done for you in the past? How can remembering those times help you when things get tough?

2. Trust what God will do.
Now read verses 17-19, since they indicate a shift in Habakkuk's focus. Because of what God had already done for His people, Habakkuk was trusting in God, no matter how things might have looked.

During Habakkuk's time, people's daily existence was dependent on crop yields and cattle health. Yet Habakkuk says that even if the figs don't blossom, the vines don't produce fruit, olives don't grow, fields don't yield food, or the flocks and the herds are nowhere to be found, he is still going to trust in God. This would be like saying, "Even if I don't have any money in the bank, any job to make money, or any place to live, I will still trust God."

How could he say something like that? He was relying on God in a way that extended beyond his circumstances. His situation was not going to determine his level of faith. He would trust in God, no matter what.

Think about it:
What are some challenges that can discourage us from living out our faith?

There is an old legend about the emperor, Augustus. He was told about a Roman citizen who was burdened with extensive debt, yet he was able to sleep soundly every night. Because of the paranoia and stress of his position, Augustus had struggled to get any sleep. When he heard about this citizen, he tried to purchase that man's bed.

I like that story, because it reminds me that even the people who appear to have it all still don't necessarily have peace. That can only come when we trust in God. In fact, Habakkuk says that God's power will make "his feet like the deer's." We have all seen how deer run, and Habakkuk is saying that God will give him that kind of strength. He is putting his trust in God.

We all have questions, and God is big enough to handle any questions we can ask. Just check out the book of Job or Psalms if you want a glimpse of people who follow God asking tough questions. Habakkuk reminds us that even when we don't understand why things are happening the way they are, we can remember what God has done and trust that He will be with us in the future, whether it makes total sense to us or not.

Looking to Jesus

When Jesus began His ministry, the Jewish people were living under the power of the Roman Empire. No longer in Babylonian exile, they were finally allowed to practice their faith as long as Rome allowed

Sharing the Prophets

it. As they waited for the promised Messiah to come, they imagined that this chosen one would lead them to victory over Rome and restore a physical kingdom. When Jesus started to perform miracles, they watched Him heal lepers and feed thousands of people with just a young boy's lunch. That sounds like a good leader in war time, doesn't it—someone who could heal wounded soldiers and provide food for everyone? No wonder some of them wanted to make Jesus king by force (John 6:15).

But Jesus' mission was different than what they had in mind. That is one reason the apostles had such a hard time understanding it. Jesus, the Son of God, was going to die? Like a criminal? That didn't make any sense. How could someone who was going to establish a kingdom be put to death on a cross? Crucifixion was a reminder to the common man not to mess with the Roman Empire. A crucifixion would prove Rome's power, wouldn't it?

Yet Jesus kept telling His apostles that He was going to suffer, be rejected, and then be put to death (Mark 8:31, for example). They didn't understand it when He predicted it, and they didn't seem to get it as the crucifixion was taking place. Yet once they saw the risen Lord, when they recognized His power over death, they began to understand the kind of kingdom that Jesus had come to establish—a spiritual one.

I can imagine that a follower of Jesus might have sounded like Habakkuk during the crucifixion, "the wicked have surrounded us; why is this happening?" Yet it was part of God's ultimate plan.

Their lack of understanding did not mean the plan was wrong, it just means they didn't yet comprehend it. In our lives, we will often experience times like that. When we do, it is good to remember two truths: We are not alone, and the same God who showed His power over death is more powerful than any challenge we might face.

Prophet Sharing

Though there was a lot Habakkuk certainly didn't know (why God was silent, why people were being denied justice, why the wicked were prospering), he was reminded of some important things in the end. Sometimes our tough questions cause us to forget some important things, too. What are some things of which you need to be reminded right now when it comes to God's identity (who He is) and His plans (what He's doing)?

John: The Baptizing PROPHET

Mystery Object: CRICKETS

It's hard not to associate John the Baptist with bugs and honey—that is, after all, what he ate.

If you really want to make your class memorable, you can buy edible crickets online. You'll probably have some students who are brave (yes, that's the word) enough to try them. (Also remember, John ate these without any seasoning!)

Ice Breakers

Option 1: Bon Appétit
If you end up going with the edible crickets, that's the only ice breaker you need! See how many of your students will actually eat a bug!

Option 2: All About Me/All About Others
See if you can get two volunteers to help you with a little roleplaying. (For the best results, talk to these two students beforehand and rehearse with them a little bit!)

Person #1 will play the role of "all about self." Person #2 will play the role of "all about others."

Say something like this to your class:
I have asked a couple of people to act out two different kinds of personalities. It's your job to figure out what kind of person each

of these actors is pretending to be. You can ask any questions you want to help figure out what kind of personality they have."

Here are a couple of example questions in case your class goes silent...

Question #1: "What did you do this weekend?"
Person #1 could say something like: "Tell me about my weekend? Man, what can I say? It's great to be me. My life is better than yours. People wish they could have weekends like I have. I decided this weekend it was time for me to get a new phone because my old one was like 3 months old, and the camera needed to be upgraded so I could take better selfies."

Person #2 could say something like: "This weekend I went my grandparents' house. I love being around them and I admire them so much. My grandma is the greatest cook, and she even made an extra meal to take to her neighbor across the street because his wife passed away recently. My grandad is an awesome storyteller. He's a good man and he works hard every day. He had a major surgery last year, and he's in pain most of the time, but he never complains. He's always asking me how things at school are going, and he tells me that he's proud of me.

Question #2: "What kinds of things do you enjoy doing?"
(Person #1 talks about themselves; Person #2: talks about helping others.)

Question #3: Tell me about your family.
(Person #1 talks about themselves the entire time and completely ignores the question. Person #2 answers the question.)

After the class has had a few minutes to get a feel for the two personalities, ask them to describe Person #1 and Person #2.

Say something like:
Have you ever met someone like Person #1, who continually makes everything about themselves? If you have a story, they have a better one. If you have an idea, theirs is always better. They seem

to be obsessed with themselves: how many "likes" they can get, how unaware that they are of what other people are going through or feeling, and so on.

The sad reality is self-centered people are a dime a dozen. They're everywhere in our society.

But you know what's hard to find? People like Person #2. People who are genuinely interested in others. People who are encouragers. People who are humble. People who don't mind if another person has the spotlight. People who understand that the world doesn't revolve around them.

Today, we're going to talk about one of the most remarkable people ever to walk the face of the earth, and one of the things that made him so remarkable was that he truly understood how important Jesus was.

Prophet Profile: John

- His mother, Elizabeth, was a relative of Mary, the mother of Jesus; thus John and Jesus were relatives. (Luke 1:36)
- Bold, powerful preacher who had a great following (he even had disciples).
- Lived in the wilderness of Judea and baptized many (including Jesus) in the Jordan River.
- Preached a message of repentance and of the coming kingdom of heaven.
- Wore clothes made from camel's hair (I'll bet that was itchy)
- Diet consisted of locusts and wild honey.
- Was compared to Elijah, the most famous of Old Testament prophets.
- Had a great understanding of the importance of Jesus, the Messiah. Consider these statements that John made of Christ:
- Said he was not even worthy to untie the strap of Jesus' sandal. (John 1:27)

- "Behold, the Lamb of God, who takes away the sin of the world!" (John 1:29)
- "And I have seen and have borne witness that this is the Son of God." (John 1:34)
- "He must increase, I must decrease." (John 3:30)
- Remained humble despite his large following; never mistook his role in pointing people toward Jesus, and rejoiced in Christ's ministry.
- Beheaded for speaking out against Herod, who divorced his own wife and took his brother's wife Heriodias.

Prophet in Action

If you have ever been to Washington D.C., you know that city is filled with monuments and statues: the Lincoln Memorial, the Washington Monument, the Vietnam Veterans Memorial Wall, to name a few. Everywhere you look, you can find a memorial designed to commemorate something or someone important. When you walk around the National Mall, you will also see crowds of tourists taking pictures or livestreaming their visits. People come from all over just to see these famous landmarks in person.

But there is one group of people that is unfazed by all this history: the tour guides. They are on hand at each of the historical sites, museums, and monuments, but they don't spend their time taking pictures. These sights are familiar to them, just part of a day's work. After a while, it would be easy to walk right by one of those memorials without a second glance.

Think about it:
What are some things you have seen or used today that you haven't given a second thought? (Examples might include air conditioning, running water, etc.)

This can happen to us as well, especially when we read about famous people in the Bible. If we see a name in Scripture, and we know we have studied about that person before, then we might be tempted to keep reading without stopping to think about what that person did. Once we think we know all there is to know about someone, we move on to someone else.

John the Baptist is one of those famous names. We remember he came before Jesus, and we might even picture him living in the wilderness, sustaining himself on a locust and honey diet. Then we move on to see who else we read about in the Gospels. But first, we need to stop and reflect on who John was and why he was important. After all, Jesus once said there was no one born who was greater than John. That is a huge compliment, and God's Word lets us know why John was worthy of it.

Read Luke 7:18-28 to find out what leads to that comment. What made John great?

His commitment made him great.

In Luke 7:24, Jesus tells the people John was not a "reed shaken by the wind." This is a biblical image for someone who is blown around by circumstances. Have you ever known someone who just goes along with the crowd and never stands up to other people? That is what this expression describes. John baptized in the Jordan River, and even today you can find long stalks of reeds along that shore. But when they saw John by the Jordan, they were not looking at someone who just went wherever the wind might blow. He stood up for truth, even when it meant facing off with a ruler.

In the beginning of the Gospels, we are introduced to Herod the Great, a paranoid ruler. By the time of John the Baptist's ministry, Herod the Great had died and his territory had been divided among three of his sons: Archelaus, Antipas, and Philip. The first two also used their father's name (Herod Archelaus and Herod Antipas), which can make things confusing.

Antipas went to visit his brother, Philip, and was immediately enamored with Philip's wife Herodias. Antipas divorced his wife and took Herodias to be his own wife. Like any king, Herod Antipas was probably surrounded by servants who flattered him and would never stand up to him. But John did.

John told Herod Antipas that it wasn't lawful for him to take his brother's wife, and he also listed other things Antipas should not have done (Luke 3:19). That landed him in prison.

After doing that, Antipas was conflicted about what to do next. Part of him wanted to put John to death, even though he was afraid of how people would react (Matthew 14:5). Yet part of him understood John's role and even enjoyed hearing him speak (Mark 6:20).

Finally, when Antipas is celebrating his birthday with a feast, his daughter dances for everyone there. Antipas impetuously promises her anything she wants, and Herodias convinces her to ask for John the Baptist's head on a platter. He can't back down in front of all his guests, so he has John beheaded. Talk about a "reed shaken by the wind"—Herod Antipas seems to make his decisions based on circumstances around him, whether it is the concern of the crowd or the plans of his wife. John does the opposite.

Think about it:
What are some things Christians must decide to do, no matter what?

John's commitment did not mean he never doubted. After all, he sent messengers to Jesus to ask if He was the Messiah, or if John should keep waiting.

This seems strange, because if anyone should know about Jesus, wouldn't it be John? Even before he was born, he leaped in his mother's womb when she greeted Mary, the mother of Jesus. He is the one who saw Jesus and announced, "Behold, the lamb of God, who takes away the sins of the world!" (John 1:29). Hadn't John said he wasn't worthy to untie the sandals Jesus wore (John 1:27)? Wasn't he the one who said he was unworthy to baptize Jesus, before doing it to fulfill all righteousness (Matthew 3:14-15)? Why would he send a message filled with doubt?

Sharing the Prophets

It is possible that John was sending his disciples to Jesus to calm their fears. He might have thought that a conversation with Jesus could ease the doubts in their mind. But I (Andrew) think it is more likely that this question expressed his own internal struggle. He was an outdoorsman, used to an active lifestyle, who was now imprisoned. He was prophesying for the Lord, but now he was in serious trouble. If Jesus was really the Messiah who could do all kinds of miracles, why was John still in prison?

Notice the way Jesus responds. He does not say, "How dare you? You should know better than anyone else who I am!" Instead, he merely tells John's disciples to report what they see. Jesus was doing miracles that fulfilled prophecy from Isaiah 35 and 61, and He knew John needed to be reminded of that.

This interaction actually gives us insight into how to deal with our own doubts. The Bible never holds back in revealing the imperfections of followers of God, and more than one dealt with doubt. So will we, if our faith is growing. How do we handle it?

We can do what John did—reflect on the blessings of God (report what we see), go back to Scripture (learn more about Jesus' mission), and above all, bring it to Jesus.

Think about it:
What are some common faith struggles for Christians? Why is it sometimes hard to bring those to God in prayer? How can working through struggles help our faith grow?

His humility made him great.

In Luke 7:25, Jesus reminds listeners that John was not a man dressed in soft clothing. That is another figure of speech that might seem strange to us, but in the ancient world, soft fabric would have been expensive. What Jesus is saying is that John was not a well-dressed, well-connected prophet who wore expensive clothes, lived in palaces, and told influential people what they wanted to hear. John understood his role.

Sharing the Prophets

Take a few minutes to read John 1:29-30 and John 3:26-30. What do those passages reveal about John's self-image?

Think about it:
Is it fun to spend time with people who only think about themselves? Why?

John was more interested in glorifying Jesus than making himself look good. Even when John's disciples were worried that Jesus' baptism statistics were better than theirs, John said, "He must increase, and I must decrease." John's joy was not made full when people looked at him, but when they looked at Jesus.

This is so different than what we tend to do. We search for joy in attention from others. We desire the rush that comes when people laugh at our jokes, compliment our clothes, or comment on our posts.

Have you ever noticed that kind of joy is short-lived? If I find my joy in how other people react to me, then soon those reactions won't make me feel better. If someone doesn't click on a picture I post or say something about what I am wearing, I will become paranoid. Why haven't they said anything? Did I do something wrong?

The positive feeling that comes from how others respond to me will never give lasting fulfillment.

Think about it:
What are some ways we are tempted to rely on the actions of others to determine our feelings?

Here is another way to think about it: In John 1, Jesus is described as the "Light." In a dark world, Jesus is the Light. John 1:8 tells us that John the Baptist was not the light, but he came to testify about the light. Later in John 5:35, Jesus describes John as a lamp that was burning and shining. This is a good contrast for us; John was a lamp, but He was not the light.

Sharing the Prophets

The same should be true for us; we shine our lamps so that people will see the light of Christ. Even in the Sermon on the Mount, when Jesus tells His followers they are the light of the world, He tells them to let their light shine so that men may see their good works and glorify the Father in heaven (5:16). The goal of shining our lights is never to draw people to us, but to draw people to God.

Think about it:
Are you trying to be a lamp or "the" light?

Walking past monuments in Washington D.C. is impressive. I am thankful for the people honored there, who lived and made sacrifices for others. Yet what Jesus says about John the Baptist is better than any memorial or statue. We have already seen that John's attitude would keep him from desiring a monument to commemorate his life, but if one were constructed, the inscription would probably mention both his commitment and his humility—two qualities that made him great.

Looking to Jesus

There are many ways we have seen other prophets point to Jesus, either by direct prophecies or by modeling a quality Jesus will display. Yet John is the most direct. His role as a forerunner meant that he would literally point others to the Messiah. When Jesus talks about him in Luke 7, He not only says that no one born of woman was greater than John, but He also says that he who is least in the kingdom of God is greater than John.

What does this mean? We are not used to thinking of "kingdoms," but this language indicates who a person is serving. If you are a part of a certain kingdom, that means you are under the authority of the king. In a sense, every follower of God in both Old and New Testaments served in His kingdom, under His rule. John certainly served God faithfully.

But kingdom language in the New Testament can also describe the church. After all, that is what Jesus came to establish, not an earthly kingdom, but a spiritual body. Jesus preached about the kingdom of God (Mark 1:14), and He told Peter he would receive the "keys to the kingdom" (Matthew 16:19). When Peter stands up in Acts 2 and preaches about Jesus, people are baptized, and the church is established. The key to the kingdom of God is the good news Peter preached.

As great as John was, he never got to see the way Jesus realized His mission and established the church. John never had the privilege of standing to listen to Peter on Pentecost or to worship with the early church. He never got to see the way God performed miracles through the apostles, and he never got to participate in standing up to the authorities to preach about Jesus alongside Peter and John. He never had the privilege of being part of the church on earth.

John was great, but being part of the kingdom of God is even greater.

Prophet Sharing

John was definitely a guy who understood his role in Jesus' story. He existed to point people toward Jesus. What about you? Who do you know right now that you need to point toward Jesus?

Anna: The PROPHETESS with Enduring Faith

Mystery Object: A PICTURE OF OLD FAITHFUL

Anna was old and full of fai ☺

Ice Breakers

Option 1: Last List

Quickly divide the class into two teams (boys against girls is always a lively competition). Give each team a piece of paper and a pen, and have them choose someone who will write down all of the team's answers.

Say something like:

Here's what your teams will be doing. You will have 60 seconds to write down as many things as possible that fit the description that I am going to give. Are you ready? Here is the category: things that last a long, long time. Go!

After the game, have each team read their answers out loud (there will probably be some debate as to whether or not the things they write down are truly long-lasting! So you be the judge!), and declare a winning team.

Say something like:

It's hard to find things that truly last, isn't it? Over time, the clothes that we wear fade, and tear, or go out of style. We love our phones but they have a relatively short shelf life. Light bulbs burn out, buildings deteriorate, and of course, you and I are temporary, too. We began dying as soon as we were born (there's an encouraging thought).

It's hard to look around and find things that last a long time, but as we will study today, Anna, a woman that the New Testament calls a prophetess, offers us a picture of just how beautiful long-lasting faithfulness is.

Option 2: You in 60 Years

Give all your students paper and a pen, and do this activity.

Say something like:

Do you ever wonder what it will be like to be old? For just a few minutes today, I want you to think about what you will look like and be like 60 years from now. Your job is to draw a picture of what you think you will be doing 60 years from now.

Give them a couple of minutes to do this, and then have them show their picture and talk about it.

Then say something like:

We are going to talk about an old woman and prophetess named Anna, and I want you to see what kind of person she was in her old age. How did she spend her time? Is she someone you would like to be like in your old age?

Prophet Profile: Anna

- Name means "favor," "grace," or "beautiful."
- Interestingly, Anna is not the only prophetess we read about in the New Testament. In the book of Acts, for example, we read that Philip had four daughters who prophesied.
- Was married for seven years, then widowed.

Sharing the Prophets

- From the tribe of Asher. Interestingly enough, in Deuteronomy, Moses prophesies of the tribe of Asher, "your strength will equal your days" (Deuteronomy 33:25). Anna's life certainly shows evidence of that!
- Could be found constantly worshiping at the temple, night and day.

Prophet in Action

It was the big event. Approximately, 105 million Americans were glued to their TVs. This was before you could set your DVR or stream a movie on your phone; people actually had to turn their televisions to the right channel at the right time to watch a show.

What could have been so compelling that 105 million Americans all stopped what they were doing to watch?

It wasn't the debut of the Beatles on the "Ed Sullivan Show." That is an historic moment in TV history, but it didn't get this many American viewers.

It wasn't the moon landing. People viewed it all over the world, but the number of Americans tuned in was smaller than 105 million.

Was it the Super Bowl? No. Super Bowls always bring in huge audiences, but this was even bigger than some Super Bowls.

It was the final episode of a TV show called "M.A.S.H." You probably haven't seen it, but it was a TV show that ran for 11 years, and it still holds the record for the largest audience to watch a finale.

Why do you think that is? Why would so many people want to see the last episode? Because endings matter.

During the 83rd running of the Indianapolis 500, Robby Gordon found out that lesson the hard way. Another racer had crashed, causing the yellow caution flag to wave. All the other lead drivers took a pit stop, but Gordon had 37 laps to go, and he thought he could make it on just one tank of fuel. With only one lap to go, however, he needed a little more and had to stop quickly to get just a little bit of fuel.

That brief stop took him from first place to fourth place. In an interview, Gordon would quote the number one rule in racing: "You must first finish before you finish first."

Endings matter.

It is always easier to start than to finish. Anyone who has ever run a 5K or started an extensive project for school knows that it is hard to come through and finish strong. Scripture gives us examples of people who started well, but didn't finish well, such as King Solomon who allowed his multiple wives to turn his heart away from God. But Scripture also shows us lives who finished faithfully, and the prophet Anna is one of those.

Read Luke 2:46-48 to find out more about her.

Think of what it took for Anna to finish well. She had experienced the death of her husband after only seven years of marriage. She had been a widow for decades by the time she was 84 years old. She remained in the temple focused on God, fasting and praying. This means she was regularly disciplining herself by focusing on God instead of other desires.

Her focus reminds us of the way Hebrews 12:1-2 describes how a Christian runs the race of faith. In that chapter, we are reminded of the "cloud of witnesses," the faithful people who surround us and encourage us as we serve God. It also tells us how we can develop a faith that endures. Two principles are important, and the prophetess Anna shows us both: an enduring faith requires laying aside and looking ahead.

Read Hebrews 12:1-2.

Think about it:
After reading this passage, what do you think Christians need to lay aside? In what way do Christians need to look ahead?

Sharing the Prophets

For our faith to endure, we must lay aside some things.

The image of a cloud of witnesses is an encouraging one. When we think of faithful people who lived before us, we might feel intimidated. After all, Abraham was willing to leave home and follow God. Moses led an entire nation of people out of slavery. Esther was willing to risk her life by entering the throne room and seeking to save her people. Have I ever done anything like that?

But the heroes of faith are not critics sitting in an audience, critiquing our performance. They are fans sitting in the bleachers, cheering us on as we run our race. It is good to know we aren't the only ones.

This is where Anna's example can inspire us. Do you think her life turned out the way she had envisioned? When her family and her husband's family gathered for their wedding (remember, weddings were a big deal in the ancient world), do you think she dreamed of years together? Did she imagine children? Did she envision growing old together with her husband? That never happened. Within a few short years, she was widowed. Yet she did not let that keep her from glorifying God.

Think about it:
Are you dealing with something in life you never planned to experience? Anna knew what that was like.

When Anna decided to spend time in the temple, she was deciding what her priorities would be. She could have allowed her grief to push her away from God, but she chose to stay close.

When we struggle, we are often tempted to turn away from God to someone or something else. In fact, one of the promises of sin is that it will deliver us from something. If I'm angry, I will feel better if I hurt someone else, right? If I'm sad, won't I improve things if I drink or take something to make me feel better?

Yet Hebrews 12 reminds us that sin does exactly the opposite of what it promises. Instead of giving us freedom, it restricts us. Satan would love for us to think that God's rules are restrictive, and that sin frees us from them, but that is not at all what happens. God's way frees us, and sin restricts us.

Have you ever talked to someone who has faced addiction? No matter what the object of addiction might be—drinking, drugs, pornography—an addict will tell you that once the temporary high wears off, you are left with a hole in your life that addiction cannot fill. Pretty soon, you feel the walls closing in, as the very thing that promised to make you feel great is now hurting your relationships, your abilities, and even your thinking.

Sin doesn't deliver on its promises. It binds and entangles us. We have to lay it aside.

For our faith to endure, we need to look ahead.

Hebrews 12 also tells us to look to Jesus, the "author" and "perfecter" of our faith. These terms might be unfamiliar to us, but the book of Hebrews has already used them to describe Jesus (Hebrews 2:10).

When we think of an author, we typically picture someone sitting at a desk, typing the pages of a book. But another way to translate this particular term is "pioneer." Jesus has gone before us, and He shows us the way.

When we think of the word *perfect*, we usually imagine a test on which we did not miss a single answer. But this word refers to a sense of completion—to "perfect" something is to "complete" it. In Hebrews 5, we find out that Jesus suffered, and through that suffering was made perfect (complete). That means He is the One who can perfect, or complete, us.

Anna shows us the life of someone constantly looking toward God. That is why when she sees Jesus for the first time, she immediately gets it. She knows who He is.

Think about how many religious leaders walked in and out of that temple all the time, passing her on the way, and they would not be able to recognize Jesus as the Messiah. They would misunderstand Him, and they would try to silence Him.

Not Anna. She had a lifetime of looking toward God, so when she saw Jesus, she knew who He was.

We focus on Jesus, and He is the ultimate example of focus. Think about all the ways Jesus shows us in the Gospels where our focus should be.

In Mark 1, when Jesus' miracles had drawn a crowd in Capernaum that was pressing in on them wherever they went, Jesus reminded His apostles He needed to preach in other towns. That was His mission.

In Luke 9:51, as the days were approaching for Jesus to ascend into heaven (which could only happen after His crucifixion and resurrection), Jesus set His face to go to Jerusalem. Think about it—Jesus knew exactly what was going to happen to Him in Jerusalem, and He still went.

We need to lay aside the sin that can entangle us, and we need to look ahead to the Savior who sets us free. That is how we can finish well, the way Anna did, and live a life that glorifies God.

Think about it:
What do you want your legacy to be? Do you have the focus in your life right now that will leave that kind of legacy? If not, how can you adjust your focus?

Looking to Jesus

In 1968, Mexico hosted the Summer Olympics. The final event in Olympic Stadium was the marathon. People had packed into the stands to watch the first athlete enter the stadium to complete his run of 26.2 miles.

Sharing the Prophets

The crowd erupted in cheers as he crossed the finish line. Runner after runner entered the stadium and crossed the finish line. Finally, after almost all of the runners had finished, the crowd began filing out of the stadium.

Only a few thousand were left an hour later, when John Stephen Akwhari limped into the stadium.

Akwhari was a Tanzanian runner whose head and muscles had begun throbbing in pain, causing him to fall to the ground. He sustained serious leg injuries, and the officials urged him to quit, but he decided to keep going. After having his knee bandaged, he hobbled the rest of the way to the finish line. Entering the stadium, he moved across the track at a painstakingly slow pace, before he finally collapsed across the finish line.

Afterward, when he was asked by a reporter why he had not simply dropped out, he responded with a memorable line that has endured over the years: "My country did not send me to start the race. They sent me to finish."

As Paul was nearing the end of his life, he wrote to his friend Timothy. Of all the letters from Paul we have in Scripture, 2 Timothy is the latest chronologically. In other words, it is the last letter we have that Paul wrote. In 2 Timothy 4:7, Paul described the result of a life spent looking to Jesus: "I have fought the good fight, I have finished the course, I have kept the faith… (NASB)" He went on to say that he knew there was a crown in store for him, a symbolic way to describe the eternal reward God promises to Christians.

Paul was not content to simply start well; He wanted to finish well. He didn't become a Christian only to start the race; He was determined to finish it.

Wherever you are in your faith, don't be content just to get off to a good start. Do what it takes to live your entire life for God, so that when you get to the place Paul was, you can say what Paul said.

Sharing the Prophets

Endings matter. Make yours one like Anna's—fight the good fight, finish the course, and keep the faith.

Prophet Sharing

Is there an area of your life in which you started out strong, but couldn't finish? Ask God for strength to help you follow through and finish strong!

www.ingramcontent.com/pod-product-compliance
Lightning Source LLC
LaVergne TN
LVHW051600080426
835510LV00020B/3070